TAIWAN'S NATIONAL SECURITY: DILEMMAS AND OPPORTUNITIES

Taiwan's National Security: Dilemmas and Opportunities

Edited by

ALEXANDER C. TAN
University of North Texas

STEVE CHAN
University of Colorado

CALVIN JILLSON
Southern Methodist University

Routledge
Taylor & Francis Group

LONDON AND NEW YORK

First published 2001 by Ashgate Publishing

Reissued 2018 by Routledge
2 Park Square, Milton Park, Abingdon, Oxon OX14 4RN
711 Third Avenue, New York, NY 10017, USA

Routledge is an imprint of the Taylor & Francis Group, an informa business

Copyright © Alexander C. Tan, Steve Chan and Calvin Jillson 2001

Notice:
Product or corporate names may be trademarks or registered trademarks, and are used only for identification and explanation without intent to infringe.

Publisher's Note
The publisher has gone to great lengths to ensure the quality of this reprint but points out that some imperfections in the original copies may be apparent.

Disclaimer
The publisher has made every effort to trace copyright holders and welcomes correspondence from those they have been unable to contact.

A Library of Congress record exists under LC control number: 2001088769

ISBN 13: 978-1-138-72806-6 (hbk)
ISBN 13: 978-1-138-72802-8 (pbk)
ISBN 13: 978-1-315-19066-2 (ebk)

Contents

List of Figures

List of Tables

About the Authors

Steve Chan is Professor and Acting Chair at the Department of Political Science, University of Colorado at Boulder.

Cal Clark is Professor at the Department of Political Science, Auburn University.

Bruce J. Dickson is Associate Professor at the Department of Political Science and Director of the Gaston Sigur Center for East Asian Studies at George Washington University.

Calvin Jillson is Professor of Political Science and Director of the John G. Tower Center for Political Studies, Southern Methodist University.

Chia-lung Lin is Assistant Professor at the Department of Political Science, National Chung Cheng University in Taiwan.

Robert A. Scalapino is Robson Research Professor Emeritus at the Department of Political Science, University of California at Berkeley.

Alexander C. Tan is Assistant Professor at the Department of Political Science, University of North Texas.

Scott Walker, Ph.D candidate at the Department of Political Science, University of North Texas.

Tsung-chi Yu, Ph.D candidate at the Department of Political Science, University of North Texas.

Preface

ALEXANDER C. TAN, STEVE CHAN, and CALVIN JILLSON

Taiwan's Security Dilemma

In the second half of the 20th century, the world witnessed the phenomenal transformation of East Asia from a collection of war-torn nation-states struggling to survive to dynamic economies that are among the world's export powerhouses. As one of the tiger economies, Taiwan's development is typical. From an economic backwater in the early 1950s, Taiwan created an economic miracle that is now one of the world's economic and export dynamos. By the year 2000, Taiwan has become a full-fledged member of the world's advanced industrial countries.

As Taiwan's economy continues to evolve and develop, the 1990s also ushered in an era of unprecedented political transformation and development in the island. Through the process of political liberalization that began under the late President Chiang Ching-kuo, and later democratization by President Lee Teng-hui, Taiwan has become a model of peaceful political transformation. In 1996, the first democratic presidential election was conducted -- a first in the five thousand years of the history of any Chinese society. In 1997, constitutional amendments have streamlined Taiwan's governmental structure to create a more competitive and efficient government. These reforms are seen by many as further steps toward a representative form of democracy. In May 2000, the transfer of power in the presidency from the Kuomintang to the Democratic Progressive Party heralded the consolidation of democracy in Taiwan.

These great strides in the past fifty years, nonetheless, belie the ever-present concern for national security and national survival that may undermine and dismantle all these achievements. In the 21st century, Taiwan is faced with a unique challenge in its attempt to achieve economic growth, stability, and political order. As part of a divided state, Taiwan's position bears no similarity to any other nation in the world.

Unlike Germany and Korea where conditions are more favorable to the democratic country of the respective dyads, the Taiwan-China dyad is characterized by so much asymmetry in land, people, size of the communist

neighbor.   In geographic and demographic terms, China is a behemoth. In economic terms, China is a much bigger economy in absolute terms -- though Taiwan is stronger in per capita terms.   Unfortunately for Taiwan, this glaring asymmetries extend to the political sphere as well. Taiwan is shut out from most significant international organizations like the United Nations.
  And as Bruce Dickson notes in his chapter in this book that while Taiwan has extensive economic and cultural ties with other countries, it only has formal political ties with 29 countries. To complicate the picture further, Taiwan's "security guarantor" -- the United States -- does not even have formal diplomatic relations with it.
        Indeed, these asymmetries and complications present significant challenges to Taiwan's policymakers.   And, in the face of China's growing power and its oft-stated threat of reunifying the island by force if Taiwan declares *de jure* independence, Taiwan threads a fine line as it asserts its rightful role in the region (and the world) and as it seeks to ensure security of the nation.   These unique circumstances provide Taiwan with both dilemmas and opportunities as it joins the community of nations in the 21st century.
        What are these dilemmas and opportunities in Taiwan's national security?   What does democratization of the polity mean for Taiwan's national security? These are some of the questions that the chapters in this volume seek to examine in depth. To examine these questions, the approach we chose is decidedly an acknowledgment of the comprehensive nature of national security, that is, we seek to examine Taiwan's economic security, national defense concerns, and the impact of domestic politics on its national security.   By taking such an approach, we break down the artificial distinction between high politics and low politics. Indeed, the dictum that "politics stops at the water's edge" -- so to speak -- no longer applies when one discusses Taiwan's national security. The blurring of these distinctions is made painfully clear by Taiwan's predicament for clearly domestic political choices have international repercussions and more importantly to the survival of the state. Restructuring and structural adjustments of Taiwan's economy does not become a simple economic decision but becomes entangled in the web of national security concern due to the continued fear of being absorbed into the PRC's political economy. And as the world has witnessed in the months leading to Taiwan's first direct presidential election in 1996 and indeed in the presidential election of March 2000, laudable movement towards democratic consolidation in Taiwan but coupled with the

complicated domestic politics associated with the rise of nativism and Taiwanese nationalism have undesired repercussions on Taiwan's security and stability in the Asia-Pacific region.

Reading through the chapters in this volume, the reader will be struck by several common themes that goes through these chapters. First, the continuing threat of the PRC using force to reunify Taiwan with China. To this date, PRC has not renounced the use of force as part of the overall plan to reunify Taiwan. To PRC officials, renunciation of the use of force would simply make Taiwan unwilling to come to the bargaining table and may send Taiwan the message that Taiwanese independence is fine. To Taiwan, on the other hand, having PRC guns pointed at it signifies that there will never be good-faith negotiation between the two-sides. Second, the democratization of Taiwan has brought increasingly vociferous domestic demands for greater international involvement is making Taiwanese politicians thread a very difficult political tightrope. On the one hand, international involvement is simply a natural extension of the growing strength and confidence of the Taiwanese political economy. On the other hand, Taiwanese politicians know that many of these efforts face an uphill battle when the PRC is actively blocking Taiwan's efforts. A third theme is the issue of multilateralism and its utility as a tool for Taiwan's security. Taiwan's national security strategy cannot discount the benefits of multilateral ties both politically and economically. It seems at least for Taiwan that through the diversification of ties -- so to speak -- whether through trade and investment will it be able to make itself an important and indispensable player in the Asia-Pacific and world political economy.

Accordingly, Taiwan's evolving domestic conditions and international status offer an opportunity to study several intriguing theoretical and policy questions. One such question stems from the perspective of two-level games which argues that international agreements require domestic ratification and at the same time, the mobilization of domestic interests can constrain a state's foreign conduct. Another question concerns the politics of issue linkages and the development of trust. Are functionalists correct in arguing that rising, trade, technical cooperation, and increasing people-to-people contact (e.g., tourism, mail flow) will spill over to political consultation and cooperation? Still a third question posed especially starkly by Taiwan's evolving reality concerns the relationship between state and society. Does democratization undermine the power of a strong state and, if so, with what implications for the island's future security and growth? Conversely, does democratic consolidation provide a stronger basis for its future political economy?

Chapter 1 by Robert Scalapino lays out the broad overview of the opportunities and challenges facing Taiwan policy-makers. Chapter 2 by Cal Clark examines how the evolution of Taiwan's democracy has affected its security situation. Chapter 3 by Chia-lung Lin seek to examine what Taiwanism is, why it arose and what is its eventual impact on Taiwan's national security. Chapter 4 by Bruce Dickson examines the politics behind Taiwan's flexible diplomacy and makes an assessment of flexible diplomacy as currently practiced. Steve Chan's chapter uses the opposing theoretical framework proposed first by Karl Deutsch and Alfred Hirschman to examine how multilateral trade within the emerging trade structure of the Asia-Pacific Economic Cooperation (APEC) can affect Taiwan's national security. Alex Tan, Scott Walker, and Tsung-chi Yu's chapter is an examination of the perceived transformation in the focus of Taiwan's national security. Calling it risk diversification, Tan et al's chapter argues that Taiwan's national security has evolved from having the United States as her security guarantor to where economic statecraft and democratic consolidation are employed as mechanisms to further integrate herself in the global economy and ensuring her national survival.

Acknowledgments

Most of the chapters in this edited book began as conference papers originally presented at the Conference on "Dilemmas and Opportunity: Taiwan's National Security in the Twenty-First Century" which was held at Southern Methodist University in April 1998. We are very grateful to the chapter authors for their patience and willingness to revise their original papers to reflect the events that have transpired since the conference was held. The professionalism and commitment of the chapter authors to this collaborative project not only made the jobs of the editors easier but made the book a much better product. To them we say "thank you."

Of course, this project would not have come to fruition if it was not for the generous support of the Taipei Economic and Cultural Office in Houston and at Southern Methodist University -- The John G. Tower Center for Political Studies and the Center for Pacific Rim Legal Studies. At the Taipei Economic and Cultural Office in Houston, we acknowledge the support and encouragement of Director Edward Feng and Mr. Chi-chia Chen. At SMU, we acknowledge the assistance of Noelle McAlpine, and Catrina Whitley.

At the University of North Texas, we thank Dawn Miller who was a tremendous help in editing and preparing the book manuscript for publication. Dawn's professionalism, hard work and unselfish assistance in the project allowed us to complete this project in a timely manner. Thanks are also due to Kirstin Howgate, Anne Keirby, Jacqui Cornish, and Cilla Kennedy at Ashgate for their commitment to this project and their assistance in the production of this book.

Alex's father unexpectedly passed away while the book was still in press. We dedicate this book to the memory of Serafin Tan Yan-ping -- an avid observer of cross-Taiwan Straits politics.

A.C. Tan
S. Chan
C. Jillson

1 Taiwan -- Opportunities and Challenges

ROBERT A. SCALAPINO

Should Taiwan not be the envy of its Asian neighbors? Its GDP increased some 5.7% in 1999, with agriculture accounting for 2.6%, industry, 33.1% and services, 64.3% of the total. Per capita GNP reached $13,248. Foreign trade amounted to U.S. $267.6 billion, with a favorable balance of $5.2 billion, down from previous balances but still the envy of many. As of mid-2000, foreign currency reserves were approximately U.S. $113.5 billion, among the highest in the world.[1] And living standards for the people of Taiwan continued to improve. Projected GDP growth for 2000, moreover, is currently 6.45%.[2]

Accounting for much of these gains is the phenomenal rise of IT industries. By the beginning of 2000, Taiwan was the third largest manufacturer of IT products in the world. Young scientists and technicians, many of them trained in American universities, are in the forefront of the ongoing technological revolution.

Success does not mean an absence of economic problems or important decisions to be made. The wavering stock market is an indication of uncertainty regarding the capacities of the Chen administration to pursue and effectuate sound policies. Moreover, with the legislature reducing the workweek and with a freeze on labor imports, strains on small and medium industries have been heightened. Proposals for increased welfare payments combined with a budget deficit raise the issue of a tax hike, rarely a popular move. Further, many of Taiwan's traditional industries are facing problems, with the question of whether market mechanisms should be allowed to prevail, or whether government support should be brought into play.

On the international front, given Taiwan's extensive dependence upon foreign markets, the health of both the East Asian and American economies remains of crucial importance. Taiwan's exports in mid-2000 reached U.S. $13.6 billion monthly, an increase of some 36.5% from the previous year. Imports were also up dramatically, with July figures being U.S. $13.47 billion, up 41.9%. Trade with China was especially dynamic, as we shall later note, making the cross-Strait relationship vital.

1

In sum, the overall economic picture for Taiwan is good, but the coming months and years will not be without economic challenges, many of them connected with politics at home and abroad.[3]

On the political front, Taiwan exemplifies a society that has moved from a tightly controlled authoritarian system to an open democracy characterized by genuine political competition, a wide range of freedoms, and the increasing primacy of law.[4] When the Kuomintang transferred its authority to Taiwan fully in 1949, the one party system was maintained, and the party itself continued to reveal the earlier influence of Leninism in its structure and methods of governance. One-man primacy in the person of Chiang Kai-shek prevailed, and no genuine political opposition was permitted.[5] Only toward the end of the 1980s were changes signalled, and Chiang's son, Chiang Ching-kuo, should be given credit for permitting a peaceful evolution, although general developmental factors -- and the desire to build a more favorable image internationally -- were important assets.

The Kuomintang, however, remained the dominant force in the early years of liberalization. Only in the mid to late 1990s were there signs of change.[6] In the elections of November 29, 1997 for county magistrates and city mayors, the Democratic Progressive Party garnered more victories than the Kuomintang, suggesting that a new political era might be at hand. That proved to be true less than three years later. In the presidential election of March 18, 2000, Chen Shui-bian won the presidency on behalf of the DPP, obtaining 39% of the votes, with James Soong, head of the newly founded People First Party receiving nearly 37%, and Lien Chan running as the Kuomintang candidate, trailing with 23%. For the first time in history, the Kuomintang had been replaced at the top of the political structure in an election that was widely acclaimed as fair, and with over 80% of the eligible electorate voting.

On closer inspection, to be sure, problems in Taiwan's democracy can be found. Corruption here as elsewhere has been deeply ingrained in the system, and indeed, was one of the key issues in the March 2000 elections. Chen promised to tackle the problem of "black gold" vigorously, and charges levelled against Soong during the campaign of sequestering KMT money for personal use were probably responsible for his failure to be elected. Long in power, the Kuomintang accumulated large amounts of money from diverse sources, and used these funds in a variety of ways to underwrite its position. Even certain important media have been KMT owned or controlled.

In systemic terms, moreover, the ROC Constitution as amended in

1997 provides for a mix of parliamentary and presidential systems. It is difficult, therefore, for a president lacking a majority in the legislature to govern effectively. The president cannot dissolve the legislature unless the latter body votes no-confidence in the premier. Moreover, while the president appoints the premier, the division of power between them is unclear.

Thus, under the current system, the risk of immobilism is genuine. The Kuomintang currently holds a majority of the 225 seats in the Legislature, with the DPP possessing only one-third of the total seats. In the absence of a coalition government -- and none is in sight at present -- an impasse between the executive and legislative branches of government is not easily avoided. The next legislative election does not take place until the fall of 2001, and undoubtedly, it will be hotly contested. Prior to that time, negotiations on key issues in an effort to reach some consensus between or among parties is essential, and realizing this, Chen has reached out, seeking a "round-table" discussion among party chairmen. The results thus far have been minimal despite a few promising signs.[7] Given the bitterness that accompanied the presidential election, and the importance of personalities in the politics of Taiwan -- as elsewhere in Asia -- effective and lasting cooperation will not be easy to achieve.

After his election, Chen strove to create a coalition at the administrative level. Cabinet posts were divided between DPP and KMT members, and apart from the two parties, a majority of cabinet appointees were independents. Thus far, however, this has not contributed greatly to support in the legislature, or harmony among parties. Chen has also sought to create a broadly representative body under Y.T. Lee to make recommendations with regard to cross-Strait policies, but the effectiveness of this body remains to be seen.

Fortunately, regional or ethnic cleavages are less significant than in many other Asian societies. Taiwan is small, with only 22.5 million people, and by the beginning of 2000, 84% of the population was Taiwanese in terms of birth, whereas only 14% were Mainland born, and 2% aborigine. The accelerating Taiwanization of Taiwan politics is thus not surprising, illustrated earlier by the election of Lee Teng-hui, the first Taiwan born president. Without exception, those born on the Mainland who have survived politically like Ma Ying-jeou, currently mayor of Taipei, and James Soong, head of the PFP, have sought to become "new Taiwanese," identifying themselves with the predominately Taiwanese electorate. Nonetheless, the cleavage of earlier times between Taiwanese and Mainlanders has not been totally eradicated, and indeed, some would argue that it has recently been revitalized. The one political party advocating early reunification, the New Party, a very minor group, is composed primarily of Mainland-born individuals.

Within the Kuomintang, moreover, there is some evidence of divisions based upon Mainlander versus Taiwanese. The insistence of PRC authorities that every individual on Taiwan accept the designation "Chinese" speaks to this issue. Beijing fears that emotional identification with China is ebbing as new generations of Taiwanese come to maturity.

Despite various economic and political problems, however, Taiwan's domestic situation at present places it among the more successful East Asian states. The major uncertainties lie in the international arena. Every Taiwan citizen is forced to ask the questions, "Who am I?", "Where do I and my society belong in the global community of nations?", and most especially, "What is my relation to the People's Republic of China -- as an individual and as a member of a separate political society?" Now and for the foreseeable future, these questions will raise complex psychological as well as economic-political issues for the Taiwan community -- and for others as well.

According to recent public opinion polls, 36.9% of the people of Taiwan consider themselves Taiwanese; 34.8% consider themselves Taiwanese and Chinese; and 23.1% consider themselves Chinese.[8] These figures clearly indicate the importance of being Taiwanese among a majority of the respondents. Attitudes toward the PRC are also instructive. More than 80% of those polled favored a continuance of the status-quo, at least for the present. Within that group, 13.8% favored a permanent status quo; 34% favored the status quo for the present; 21.5% favored the status quo now, unification later; 10.7% favored the status quo now, independence later. Only 3.1% favored reunification as soon as possible.

When asked whether the "One Country, Two Systems" formula could serve to solve the problem of Taiwan-Mainland relations, 74.5% said no, 6.2% said yes. Finally, when asked whether foreign ties should be developed even if this effort led to tension in cross-Strait relations, 71% said yes, 15.6% said no.

One can always question the accuracy of such surveys and changes in attitudes are certainly possible. But recent political events and trends within Taiwan would appear to support the validity of these figures. In sum, the consciousness of being Taiwanese is strong among most citizens of

Taiwan; the overwhelming majority support a continuance of the status-quo, at least for the present; the "One Country, Two Systems" formula for reunification proffered by the PRC has very limited support; and the course of "pragmatic diplomacy" pursued by the Taiwan government is strongly approved despite its risks.

How do these results correlate with the recent course of Taiwan-PRC relations and present trends? First, semi-official negotiations between the two, through the Association for Relations Across the Strait (ARATS) and the Straits Exchange Foundation (SEF), first inaugurated in 1993, were broken off in June, 1995, after the U.S. visit of President Lee Teng-hui. They have not been resumed despite exhortations by both sides.

Moreover, the election of Chen Shui-bian was unquestionably a cause of deep concern in Beijing. The DPP had been founded to fight for Taiwan independence, and Chen had been one of its foremost spokesmen for many years.[9] While in the recent past, he has altered his views, at least publicly, few in the PRC believe that either he or his party have changed their fundamental position. Indeed, the absence of trust on both sides remains a crucial obstacle to the improvement of relations.

At this point, a brief exposition of the background of the central issue in contention between the Mainland and Taiwan, namely, the "One China" principle, is essential. When negotiations between ARATS and SEF opened in the early 1990s, they were supposedly based on an agreement reached in 1992 that the One China principle would apply. Taiwan was subsequently to insist that each side reserved the right to have its own interpretation of that principle. However, the PRC argued that agreement had been achieved on the principle that "One China" be understood to include an acceptance of Taiwan as a part of China. On certain occasions later, however, a more flexible position was advanced unofficially. At one point, Wang Daohan, ARATS head, appeared to suggest that a precise definition of "One China" might be left open. Tang Shubei, Wang's associate, also said that negotiations did not require that Taiwan first recognize the present PRC central government in accepting the One China principle. Yet there was no change in Beijing's official stance that Taiwan must accept the principle of one China, with Taiwan a part of China as a precondition for the resumption of ARATS-SEF talks.

Meanwhile, the Lee government had advanced its own interpretation of "One China." It asserted that this term related to an historical, geographical, and cultural China, but within this China, there were presently two separate political entities, each with jurisdiction over its territory; hence, dialogue should be conducted between equals, not based on a superior-subordinate relationship, with full political rights retained by both sides.[10]

The latter position symbolized a certain shift in the views of the Kuomintang, in part a reflection of the process of Taiwanization that had taken place. The official Kuomintang position was that while eventual reunification remained a goal, this could occur only when Mainland China had become a truly democratic society. Meanwhile, Taiwan was a sovereign state.[11] The latter position was expressed by virtually every high KMT official, including President Lee Teng-hui who subsequently advanced the thesis that Mainland-Taiwan negotiations should be based on "a special state to state" relationship. Not surprisingly, PRC officials condemned Lee as a "secret independence supporter," and conducted an unrelenting campaign against him.

If in its pronouncements and policies, the Kuomintang appeared to veer toward separatism, by the end of the 1990s, the Democratic Progressive Party had moved toward moderating its original stance as an advocate of declaring independence. The position subsequently held by a majority of DPP leaders was to assert that Taiwan was already independent; hence, there was no need to center attention on that issue. The question of Taiwan's future could be submitted to the citizenry in a plebiscite, allowing them to decide on the relation of Taiwan to the PRC. It was suggested, moreover, that the wording of the proposal would not be "Should Taiwan be independent?" but "Do you want Taiwan unified with the People's Republic of China?" Were this to be the wording, no one could be in doubt about the result, it was privately stated.[12]

The issue of relations with the Mainland subsequently caused fissures in both major parties. Within the KMT, a faction favoring more vigorous efforts on behalf of reunification broke away to form the New Party. As noted earlier, this party has had very limited support. Within the KMT itself, the trend was toward lessened enthusiasm for the resumption of SEF-ARATS talks or new measures to promote economic-cultural relations. Lee espoused a policy of "no haste, be patient," and urged Taiwan businessmen to look more to Southeast Asia. Restrictions were placed on investments over U.S. $50 million, and caution was also displayed with respect to opening direct transport and communication channels to the Mainland. The fear was that in-depth economic intercourse between Taiwan and the Mainland would provide the PRC with leverage which it could use against Taiwan at its discretion.

Lee's exhortations, however, had little effect upon the Taiwan business community. Taiwan trade and investment with the Mainland continued to expand rapidly, as has been noted. In 1999, Taiwan-China bilateral trade amounted to U.S. $25.8 billion according to estimates of the ROC Mainland Affairs Council, with China being Taiwan's second largest export market, next to the United States. Taiwan was also China's second largest importer, next to Japan. Further, according to Taiwan figures, Taiwanese companies had invested a total of U.S. $14.5 billion in China, with PRC figures being much higher.[13] ROC official statistics indicated that some 43% of Taiwan's overseas investment was going to the PRC as of 1998.[14] Taiwan businessmen continued to find such regions as Guangdong, Fujian and Hong Kong attractive, especially after the onset of the economic crisis in Southeast Asia.

On the political front, Taiwan under Lee suggested that when dialogue was resumed, the initial concerns should be those of procedural, economic and related matters, not political issues. PRC spokesmen, on the other hand, continued to insist that discussions deal from the outset with political matters, including the issue of reunification.

This was the situation in the spring of 2000 as the presidential campaign got underway. Despite the PRC's February White Paper with its warning that China would not wait indefinitely for reunification talks, the issue of cross-Strait relations did not dominate the domestic debates. All candidates hastened to assert that they would not be intimidated by Beijing, but most references to a future dialogue with the PRC were vague and cautionary.

Once Chen was elected, some quarters worried that much greater tension would erupt across the Strait. The new President, however, took a very moderate position, asserting that he had no intention of declaring independence, changing the ROC Constitution, or adopting other measures that might block the resumption of SEF-ARATS talks. Further, he indicated that he favored increased trade and investment between the Mainland and Taiwan, and to this end, promoted the initiation of the Three Links -- direct postal, transport, and communications facilities. It was now the PRC's turn to drag its feet, insisting that the opening of the Three Links had to be connected with a resumption of the ARATS-SEF dialogue based on acceptance of One China. Nonetheless, economic ties flourished, with approved investment valued at U.S. $3.59 billion in the first six months of

2000, and trade also showing extensive increases, as has been noted. PRC criticisms of certain businessmen for having supported Chen temporarily cast a shadow over the scene, but there were indications that such criticisms would not be continued, at least for the present.

On the political front, however, an impasse remained despite Chen's efforts. The PRC initially asserted that "We will listen to the words and observe the actions of Taiwan's new leader and wait and see in which direction he takes cross-Strait relations." In this statement, and subsequently, neither Chen nor his position was referred to by name, and Beijing asserted that the election did not alter the fact that Taiwan was a part of Chinese territory.[15]

In the weeks and months that followed, Chen made repeated efforts to display a moderate position on the issue of One China and renewed negotiations. At one point, in talking informally with a group from the Asia Foundation in June, he indicated that negotiations could be renewed on the basis of the 1992 Agreement, with the implication that at that time, the One China principle had been accepted by both sides. Under immediate pressure from within his own party, Chen retreated to the position that the two sides should embrace "the spirit of 1992," and indicated that each side had its own interpretation of One China. Shortly thereafter, the DPP in a party meeting, declined to amend its constitution -- a document that called for the independence of Taiwan. Thus, the DPP Constitution and the ROC Constitution (which defined Taiwan as the Republic of China) express significantly different positions on the crucial issue of Taiwan's status.

Meanwhile, more general political developments in Taiwan provided additional complications. Thus far, there has been very limited cooperation among Taiwan's parties on either domestic or foreign policies, as noted earlier. With Lee Teng-hui's position as party leader taken by Lien Chan, the defeated KMT candidate, the party mood thus far has not been one of assisting Chen Shui-bian and his minority government. James Soong is still pondering his future course, and that of his party, with a possibility that he will seek to play a moderator role -- but with no current indication that he will join the government. Recently, moreover, the Chen government has fallen into difficulty with the electorate, with lowered poll ratings amidst charges of incompetence and belated reform efforts.

The PRC has not been loathe to take advantage of the cleavages in the Taiwan domestic scene. Its initial political invitation after the election was to a ten-person delegation from the pro-reunification party, the New

Party. This was the first time that a Taiwan political party as a group had been invited to the Mainland. Soon thereafter, a 26-member delegation from the Kuomintang made a visit, with Vice Premier Qian Qichen telling them that based on the principle of One China, the two parties could hold talks and have consultation as equals over political differences.[16] The PRC welcomed meetings with all parties and groups opposing Taiwan independence, Qian asserted. Thus far, the DPP as a party has received no invitation, nor has its leader although DPP Mayor Frank Hsieh of Kaohsiung visited the mayor of Xiamen, the PRC's special economic zone, prior to his election as party chairman.

In sum, the evidence indicates that the PRC is now reaching out to a widening element of Taiwanese society, going beyond the business community and in the political arena, even allowing contact with select DPP figures. Yet the basic message has not been altered: One China, with Taiwan a part of China, and One Country-Two Systems -- these key elements of Jiang Zemin's earlier eight points, first enunciated in 1995, remain Beijing's bottom line.

In this setting, the position of the major nations, and especially the United States, is crucial. In the initial period after Nationalist defeat in 1949, the U.S. accepted the fact of Communist victory, and elected to withdraw from further involvement in the Chinese civil war. However, the North Korean assault on the South, and China's entry into the Korean War radically changed U.S. policies. Patrol of the Strait and military aid to the ROC on Taiwan ensued. Once again, the United States was deeply involved with respect to the Taiwan issue.

By the time of the Kissinger and Nixon visits to the People's Republic of China in 1971 and 1972, events had produced another change of major proportions. The U.S. and the PRC now had a strong mutual interest in deterring the Soviet Union. Thus, the first of the three communiques was issued in Shanghai on February 27, 1972, with the United States stating that it "acknowledges" that "all Chinese on either side of the Taiwan Strait maintain there is but one China and that Taiwan is a part of China. The United States Government does not challenge that position."[17] It was also asserted that the U.S. had an interest in a peaceful settlement of the issue by the Chinese themselves, and that the ultimate objective was the withdrawal of all U.S. forces and military installations from Taiwan as tension diminished.

Nonetheless, U.S. recognition of the Republic of China on Taiwan continued. Only on January 1, 1979 under the Carter administration were official U.S.-PRC diplomatic relations established, with the ROC no longer recognized in homage to the One China principle. However, the Taiwan Relations Act, passed by the Congress and signed by the President at the same time, provided for the sale of such defensive military equipment and services to Taiwan as might be necessary for it to maintain a sufficient self-defense capability. Moreover, unofficial relations with the ROC continued through the creation of the American Institute of Taiwan and similar Taiwan offices in Washington and elsewhere.

Thus, for the past twenty years, American policy has had elements of contradiction and ambiguity, with an effort to align U.S. statements and actions with both the Three Communiques and the Taiwan Relations Act. In June, 1998, President Clinton outlining U.S. policies toward China, defined them under the label of the Three Nos: No two Chinas, no one Taiwan-one China, and no support for a declaration of Taiwan independence. Although Clinton's speech was delivered in Shanghai rather than Beijing, some observers regarded it as a stronger tilt toward the PRC position than at any point in the past despite the administration's insistence that it was in line with previous statements.

Subsequently, however, on July 10, a few weeks after Clinton's Shanghai address, the Senate passed a resolution reaffirming U.S. commitments under the Taiwan Relations Act and supporting the membership of Taiwan in the International Monetary Fund and other international economic organizations.[18]   Efforts to approve augmented defense commitments to Taiwan were also introduced in the Congress. Clearly, the political divisions within the U.S. on the issue of Taiwan have remained extensive.

In July, 1999, Clinton defined the "three pillars" of U.S. policy as support for the One China policy, cross-Strait dialogue and a peaceful resolution of China-Taiwan differences.[19] Meanwhile, despite the pledge in the 1982 Communique to keep the quantity and quality of arms sold to Taiwan to the level existing at the time of PRC recognition, and to look toward their reduction and final termination, U.S. arms sales continued to reflect estimated Taiwan defense needs in the light of China's military modernization program.[20]

Once again, differences between the Clinton administration and the Congress were often apparent, with strong Congressional sentiment for greater support of Taiwan. Taiwan, moreover, had developed a powerful lobby to advance its case, and with its image greatly strengthened among the American people as democratization advanced, its voice was heard clearly.

Meanwhile, the U.S. maintained a policy of conscious ambiguity as to what it would do should China resort to force against Taiwan. It was repeatedly stated that the U.S. would regard the use of force, absent any formal declaration of Taiwan independence, as a grave matter. Moreover, in the aftermath of the PRC's White Paper of February, 2000, in which Beijing indicated that it would not wait indefinitely for Taiwan to agree to resume negotiations based on the principle of One China, Clinton issued a statement that the U.S. continued to make absolutely clear that the issues between the two parties must be resolved peacefully "and with the assent of the people of Taiwan."

Some Americans have favored a more precise statement with respect to U.S. policy, arguing that to avoid miscalculation, the U.S. government should state unequivocally that it will aid Taiwan militarily if it is attacked. However, this appears to be a minority view in official circles. To make a categorical statement of support might aid the Taiwan independence movement and it would certainly raise a new barrier in U.S.-PRC relations. At least equally important, it would deeply split the American public and Congress.

Thus, the United States will continue to counsel both parties to avoid actions provoking a crisis. Shortly after Taiwan's March 2000 election, that position was voiced forcefully in Taipei by a high-level unofficial delegation headed by former Defense Secretary William Perry. Reportedly, Perry told Taiwan leaders that the United States would probably not defend Taiwan should the government declare independence. According to some sources, President Chen's moderate approach to cross-Strait issues has been deeply influenced by the desire to cultivate American support. At the same time, Taiwan will continue to seek more technologically advanced weaponry from the U.S., arguing that it must meet PRC military advances.[21]

Meanwhile, the U.S. has also been urging Beijing to avoid a return to any policy of threat and intimidation, and to consider the impact of expanded missile placement on the China coast opposite Taiwan. For its part, China's concerns center not only on U.S. sales of more sophisticated military equipment to Taiwan, but also upon the U.S. development of a Theater Missile Defense (TMD) system and the possible inclusion of Taiwan in this program, as well as plans for National Missile Defense (NMD).

Clearly, the Taiwan issue will remain central in US-PRC relations.

Japan, the other significant major power close to the Taiwan scene does not face the same degree of involvement as the United States since it has no military commitments to Taiwan. Yet it is by no means aloof from the issues, given its historical connections and current ties. Whether in political-strategic or economic terms, Japan has been involved with Taiwan for more than a century.

Its recent policies have been in line with a One China doctrine, but like others, it has maintained significant economic and cultural ties with Taiwan, and attitudes among the Taiwanese are generally friendly toward Japan, in contrast to many others in East Asia. Generally speaking, Japan's colonial era did not leave a negative image here. Whether Japan would allow its bases to be used in the event of a PRC-U.S. confrontation is unclear, but the revised security guidelines promulgated in 1997 extended Japan's strategic commitments, albeit, limited in nature, to areas in the vicinity of Japan, an appropriately vague description that might include the Strait. In any case, Beijing was deeply unhappy with the possibility that Japan's interests and obligations were being implicitly extended to Taiwan by the new guidelines, and this issue has not been resolved to its satisfaction.

In any case, relations among the United States, China, and Japan will be a crucial variable in determining the future peace and prosperity of East Asia, including Taiwan. At present, despite Taiwan, the shadow of the Tiananmen Incident, and a number of other issues, U.S.-PRC relations are relatively good, with the leaders of both nations understanding the importance of working together on certain key problems. China's relations with Japan remain delicate despite extensive economic ties, with the historical legacy still weighing heavily. Yet recurrent efforts are being made to improve relations, acknowledging once again their importance.

Meanwhile, China is moving into ever greater interdependence with the Asia-Pacific region, especially in economic terms. At the same time, its political evolution is in the direction of authoritarian-pluralism despite occasional retreats. Politics is still controlled by a single dominant party and liberties restricted, but a civil society apart from the state is emerging, and the economy is mixed, with the market playing an ever more substantial role. Such a China is not democratic, as Americans or citizens of Taiwan would define democracy but it is significantly different from the Maoist era, offering greater opportunity for meaningful dialogue. In this, there is hope.

The ability to avoid a conflict in the cross-Strait relationship will be crucial to China's relations with both nations, as has been noted. Hence, it is necessary to return to that crucial issue. In the near term, there seems little likelihood of the use of force by China, assuming no extreme provocation on the part of Taiwan. Because of both its economic gains and its problems, the PRC has every reason to concentrate on domestic issues -- further economic development and political institutionalization. To become engaged in a military confrontation with Taiwan -- or with others -- would jeopardize its economic program throughout the region, and could only be a "lose-lose" formula.

To be sure, nationalism is once again at high-tide in China, and the insistence upon unrestricted sovereignty and the defense of all territorial claims is vigorous. To make China "rich and strong", and to "reunify the motherland" are powerfully appealing themes. At a time when the popular interest in ideology in its Marxist-Leninist-Maoist form has weakened, nationalism is a logical weapon in the effort to build unity and support.

However, there is another factor operating against conflict in the near future. China's military force, while in the process of being modernized, is still far behind that of the United States in all but quantitative terms, and not up to the seizure of Taiwan. Taiwan's military forces, while comparatively small, are modern, and would exact an heavy price on any would-be invader. To be sure, incidents in the Strait or with respect to the off-shore islands, or a partial blockade could unfold, and Taiwan's economic stability would probably be adversely effected. Yet with economic interdependence steadily growing, the price paid by the Mainland would also be high.

In addition, conflict would greatly damage China's recent efforts to improve relations with all of its neighbors. The PRC has promoted numerous high level visits, signed many joint communiques underlining cooperation, and pledged to live by the Five Principles of Peaceful Coexistence. In the event of unremitting threats or recurrent incidents relating to Taiwan, the existing suspicions about China's future intentions -- by no means absent in East and South Asia -- would have been fortified.

If conflict in the short term seems unlikely, however, the medium to long term prospects are less clear. President Jiang Zemin is already under pressure from more militant elements, with the allegation that he is "too weak" in asserting China's sovereignty and "standing up to the American hegemonists." If domestic conditions in the PRC create increasing fissures at both public and official levels, and if the military assume heightened authority in the security realm, greater risks might be taken with respect to Taiwan at some point in the future, especially if the political impasse continues.

What can be done to forestall such a development? There are no clear answers to this question at present, and no agreement, either in the PRC or in Taiwan, as to precisely what is desirable and possible.

The easiest steps lie in the unofficial arena. The expansion of economic ties seems certain, and with growing interdependence should come a mutual interest in stable conditions promoting trade and investment. To be sure, the threat of using economic relations as leverage cannot be dismissed, but as noted, the damage from such a course would fall on the PRC, and especially the coastal provinces, as well as on Taiwan. It seems very likely that both the PRC and Taiwan will enter the World Trade Organization shortly despite the current issue of the appropriate designation for Taiwan. WTO membership should expand the opportunities for economic interaction between the two parties, and in the long run, benefit both, despite the likelihood of some short-term challenges for the PRC.

Meanwhile, wide-ranging cultural exchanges would provide an opportunity for each side getting to know each other better. As has been noted, tourists from Taiwan visiting the PRC have numbered in the millions, with more than eleven million visas issued by 1998. There is no indication that these visits have had an adverse political impact, either on the Mainland or at home. If tourists from the PRC were permitted to visit Taiwan as well as the select academics and businessmen now going there, new links would be fashioned.

Most important might be the building of semi-official links of an informal nature, below the top ARATS-SEF level, individuals meeting at various places to discuss issues until agreement on the resumption of a fully official dialogue is reached. Such links have existed in the past, sometimes secretly, and they have served an important purpose.

Can there be agreement on the principle of One China, and to what extent is that essential? Logically, the agreement most likely to be achieved would be that of accepting the One China principle without further definition, leaving each side the right to have its own interpretation. Another approach would be that of accepting "the spirit of 1992," leaving open the controversy over whether a consensus on One China was reached at that time. In sum, in a situation like that of Mainland-Taiwan relations at present, vagueness has certain advantages over an insistence upon specificity. As long as Beijing insists that acceptance of One China must include acceptance of Taiwan as a part of China and China to be defined as the PRC, no political authority in Taiwan can agree since Taiwan is now a democracy and such a view has very limited support among the Taiwan citizens.

At some point, could a broader formula be devised that included the idea of Commonwealth or Confederation, setting aside the issue of sovereignty temporarily, and established as a means of creating a relationship that would permit full discussion of issues, possibly with the proviso that this system would be reviewed after one decade, with further determinations made? Connected with this might be an agreement that the PRC would abjure the use of force in exchange for Taiwan agreeing to pledge no declaration of independence. Even if such a formula is not acceptable at present, it -- and similar proposals -- should be put on the table for recurrent consideration.

Whatever means are used to end the current impasse, domestic developments in both societies will be of crucial importance, as noted earlier. If China becomes more open economically and increasingly market-oriented, and if its political system evolves so as to encourage freer expression and political choice, compatibility with Taiwan will grow, and with it, expanded opportunities for meaningful intercourse at all levels. If Taiwan can avoid political instability and immobilism, achieving greater cohesion and capacity to effectuate policies, it will present itself to the Mainland as an entity to be taken seriously.

Looking at the broader picture, given the delicate situation in cross-Strait relations that currently exists, the neighboring nations, large and small, have important responsibilities. Despite the PRC contention that the Taiwan issue is a purely domestic matter, the fact is that it involves the Asia-Pacific region as a whole. Were hostilities to break out, it would be far more than a domestic matter. Even incidents are of grave concern, as was illustrated by certain events of the past.

The first responsibility lies in the need for all states to accept the realities -- a Taiwan that has an economic and political system separate from the PRC and a society having extensive economic involvement throughout the region. This situation must not be changed by force, and every Asian government should put their views on this matter on the public record. At the same time, Taiwan authorities should continue to be cautioned against a formal declaration of independence, although that possibility seems far less likely, given changes in DPP policy.

Further, while the nations of the region have uniformly declared their support for the One China principle, and recognized the PRC as China, they should support the admission of Taiwan into all international organizations in which statehood is not a requirement. If such policies were to be upheld, the current American policies would receive regional support, strengthening the prospects for peace. Meanwhile, all nations including the U.S. should make every effort to keep relations with China as positive as possible, recognizing that there will always be differences to be negotiated. Wherever possible, China should be brought into a concert of powers focused on the resolution of specific issues. Moreover, it should be made clear to China that its international image is crucial, especially in democratic societies where the opinions of the electorate count. Fortunately, Beijing authorities now appear to appreciate this fact far more than in the past.

Finally, one basic trend in international relations today will have a strong influence on the cross-Strait relationship. In the years ahead, the tasks for all nations will be to meld unilateralism, bilateralism, and multilateralism in an age of growing interdependence. The broad trend is toward increasing the role of multilateralism, despite the understandable reluctance of certain states to abandon unilateralism when national interests are perceived to be at stake, or to weaken their bilateral ties, so critical in the security realm. On balance, multilateralism will serve the cause of peace, economic development and cultural understanding. Hopefully, the relationship between the PRC and Taiwan can benefit from a more integrated Asia-Pacific, including the strengthening of official sub-regional security dialogues, both bilateral and multilateral. Thus, despite the current cross-Strait political impasse, there is reason for cautious optimism.

Notes

1.   These figures are from *National Statistics*, Government of Taiwan, ROC, updated July, 2000.
2.   See *Taipei Journal*, August 4, 2000, p. 3.
3.   Various perspectives on Taiwan's economic development are presented in Joel D. Aberbach, David Dollar, and Kenneth L. Sokoloff, eds., *The Role of the State in Taiwan's Development*, M.E. Sharpe, Armonk, New York, 1994.
4.   For an earlier, generally favorable account of Taiwan's political evolution, see John F. Copper, *Taiwan--Nation-State or Province?*, Westview Press, Boulder, Colorado, 1990.
5.   An early, highly critical evaluation of Kuomintang rule is George H. Kerr, *Formosa Betrayed*, Houghton Mifflin, Boston, 1965. For later analyses, see Ralph N. Clough, *Island China*, Harvard University Press, Cambridge, 1978; F. A. Lumley, *The Republic of China Under Chiang Kai-shek*, Barrie and Jenkins, London, 1978; and

John F. Copper, *Taiwan--Nation-State or Province?*, Westview Press, Boulder, 1990.

6.   An insightful analysis of the role of the press in advancing Taiwan's democracy is Daniel K. Berman, *Words Like Colored Glass--the role of the Press in Taiwan's Democratization Process*, Westview Press, Boulder, 1992.

7.   In early August 2000, Lien Chan, chairman of the Kuomintang visited DPP headquarters, and conversed with Frank Hsieh, newly elected chairman of the Democratic Progressive Party. See "Lien-Hsieh meeting could spark cooperation," *Taipei Journal*, August 11, 2000, p. 1.

8.   These figures and the poll results that follow were presented in the *Mainland Affairs Council News Briefing*, Taipei, December 15, 1997.

9.   A detailed account of Chen Shui-bian's background and views is set forth in Richard C. Kagan, *Chen Shui-bian--Building A Community and A Nation*, Asia-Pacific Academic Exchange Foundation, Taipei, 1998.

10.   Lee's views are extensively set forth in Lee Teng-hui, *The Road to Democracy--Taiwan's Pursuit of Identity*, PHP Institute, Tokyo, 1999.

11.   In the words of Vice President Lien Chan, "we shall not pursue Taiwan independence" but "our country has always been a sovereign state"...it is premature to talk about unification because "mainland China is still not a free and democratic society, and the wealth in the mainland's possession is not equitably distributed among the people under its control" ...however, "we need neither confrontation nor retaliation..." *The Free China Journal*, January 9, 1998, p. 1.

12.   A conversation in 1998 between this author and a leading DPP figure.

13.   For these and other trade and investment figures, see an unpublished paper by Rong-I Wu, August 11, 2000.

14.   For these figures, see an interview with MSAC Chairman Chang King-yuh carried in *Sinoramao*, February 1999, pp.114-121. and "Future in cross-Straits trade," *China Daily*, February 4, 1998, p.4.

15.   For a report on the PRC's initial reactions to Chen's victory, see Elisabeth Rosenthal, "Beijing Says it Will Wait to See How Victor Acts," *The New York Times*, March 19, 2000, p. 14.

16.   See "'One-China' key to cross-Straits talks," *China Daily*, July 18, 2000, p. 2.

17.   See Paul H. Tai, ed., *United States, China, and Taiwan--Bridges for a New Millennium*, Southern Illinois University, Carbondale, Illinois, 1999, p. 256.

18.   For the texts, see Tai, ed., *op. cit*, pp. 262-265.

19.   An analysis of this statement and other U.S. policy positions is given by Ralph N. Clough in an unpublished paper, "The U.S. View of Taiwan's Future," August, 2000.

20.   See Dennis Van Vranken Hickey, *United States-Taiwan Security Ties: From Cold War to Beyond Containment*, Praeger, Westport, CN, 1994.

21.   The two recent analyses of Taiwan's security policies and the implications for the U.S. are Michael D. Swaine, *Taiwan's National Security, Defense Policy, and Weapons Procurement Processes*. RAND, Santa Monica, 1999, and Bernice Lee, *The Security Implications of the New Taiwan*, Adelphi Paper 331, IISS, Oxford University Press, Oxford, 1999.

2 Successful Democratization in the ROC: Creating a Security Challenge

CAL CLARK

The recent democratic transition of the Republic of China on Taiwan (ROC) appears extremely successful -- a "political miracle," if you will, to match Taiwan's earlier, much touted "economic miracle." The transition itself was smooth and rapid; and the country preserved institutional stability, seemingly quite easily. Across the political spectrum, leaders and citizens appear quite proud of Taiwan's becoming the first democracy in 5,000 years of Chinese society and display little sympathy for Lee Kuan Yew's or Jiang Zemin's championing of an "Asian democracy" that restricts western-proclaimed political rights as incompatible with indigenous Asian cultures.[1]

Yet, democracy, desirable as it may be, does not necessarily solve all of a society's problems. Indeed, many expected that democratization would polarize the polity over the pressing issue of national identity, thereby provoking civil strife and perhaps a confrontation with the People's Republic of China (PRC). This chapter, hence, examines how the evolution of Taiwan's democracy has affected its security situation. It begins with a synopsis and model of democratization in the ROC. The second section then describes several theoretical perspectives which imply that democratization in Taiwan might have been expected to set off a security threat by raising and polarizing the interlinked issues of national identity and cross-Strait relations. The final section reviews the evidence and argues that democracy in Taiwan has actually worked to ameliorate or dampen conflict over national identity and that the only danger that this holds for the security of the Republic of China comes from the misperception of Taiwan's domestic politics by the PRC.

Democratic Transition and Consolidation in the ROC

Many theorists interested in democracy have noted that this form of government has historically been much more prevalent in rich countries than in poor ones. This led to the argument that there may be "social requisites" for democracy. In particular, attention was focused upon how industrialization and economic development created an educated middle class to fill the expanding number of managerial and professional jobs. Such a middle class, it was assumed, should become increasingly resentful and intolerant of authoritarian political controls and, hence, exert pressure for political liberalization. This has been termed the "modernization model" because the key factor was assumed to be the rejection of "traditional" norms of deference by an educated populace.[2] This approach has received considerable criticism, especially that it is far too simplistic and mechanistic. Recent democratic transitions, for example, appear to have resulted primarily from political "settlements" at the elite level.[3] Advocates of both perspectives can point to Taiwan's democratization as a case that supports their approach, although this is somewhat ambiguous for modernization theory.

The question of whether Taiwan's historical experience is consistent with this "modernization model" can be argued either way, depending upon one's perspective on time. On the one hand, as sketched in Figure 2.1, rapid economic growth produced a sizeable middle class which was clearly pushing for greater political liberalization by the 1980s. On the other hand, however, democratization did not occur until Taiwan had reached a fairly high level of development (arguably much later than modernization theory would predict); and elite interactions were key in the actual institutional reforms that did occur.[4] In addition, Taiwan's economic dynamism is often attributed, not to the assimilation of modern western values, but to aspects of traditional Chinese culture.[5]

Overall, the combination of the ruling Nationalist or Kuomintang (KMT) Party's development policies and a Chinese society energized by a strong commitment to education and entrepreneurship produced an extremely dynamic economy and, by the 1980s, a growing middle class society.[6] A combination of initiatives from KMT reformers, pressure from the political opposition, and the demands of a well-educated citizenry then resulted in the democratization reforms of the late 1980s and early 1990s which laid the foundation for a more stable and institutionalized form of government.[7] Yet,

Figure 2.1 Overview of Taiwan's Democratization

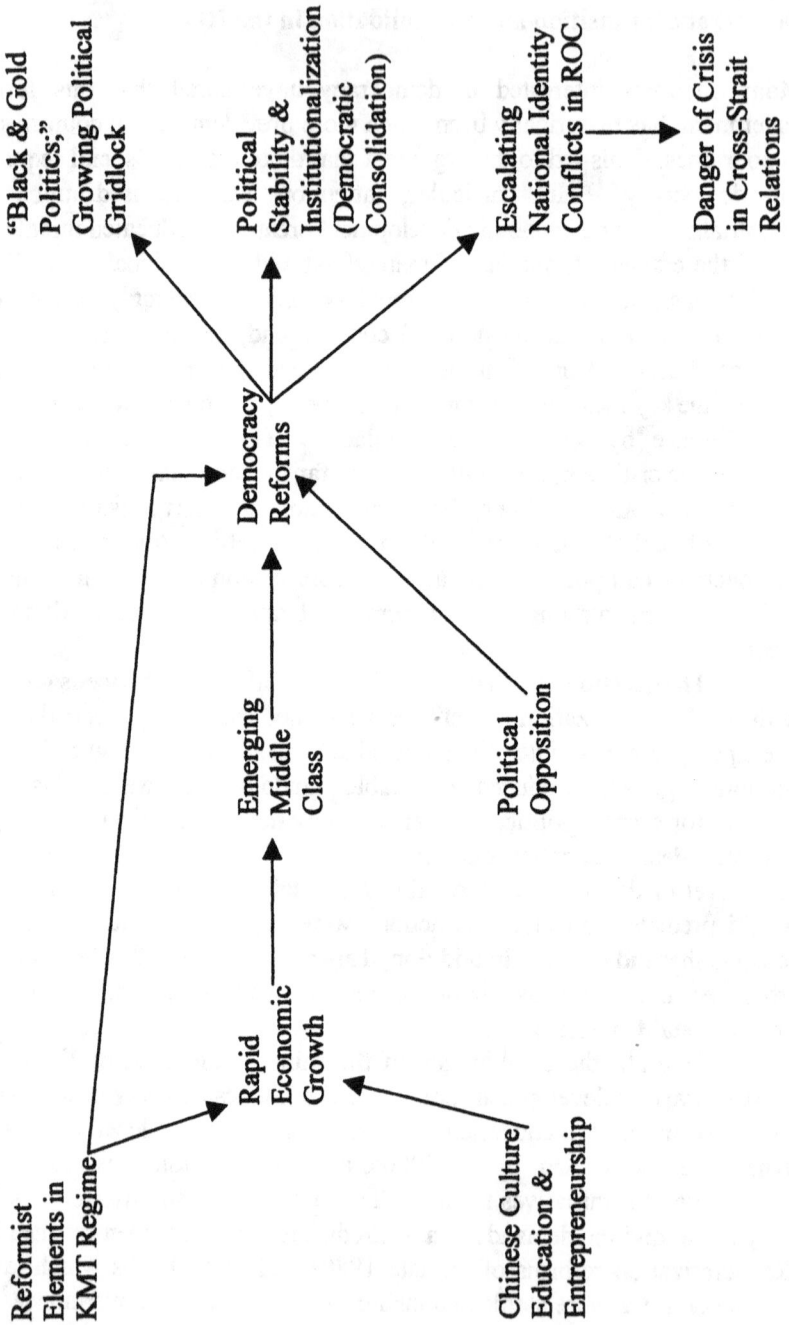

Figure 2.1 also indicates that it is too early to conclude that democratization on Taiwan means that "they all lived happily ever after." Internally, political reform has brought rising corruption and policy gridlock; externally, the growing debate over "national identity" evidently provoked serious fears among Beijing's leaders, thereby setting off the Taiwan Strait crises of 1995-1996 and 1999-2000[8] consistent with the expectation (and fears) that democracy could stimulate a security threat for the ROC.

Figure 2.1 also suggests a more complex "structural" explanation for Taiwan's ultimate democratization. This is that the authoritarian Kuomintang regime which evacuated to Taiwan at the end of the Chinese Civil War established several institutions that over time generated increased pressures for political reform.[9] Chiang Kai-shek set up something of a hybrid regime. It certainly retained strong repressive controls. The Mainlander minority (e.g., those who had come to Taiwan from China with the KMT in the late 1940s) of about 15% of the population monopolized the top leadership positions but had clearly strained relations with the Islander majority (i.e., long-time Han Chinese residents of the island) following the brutal Nationalist administration of the island after retrocession from Japan that culminated in the "2-28" uprising of 1947 which resulted in 10,000 - 20,000 deaths. Thus, the Kuomintang feared and vigorously and viciously suppressed both communists and Taiwanese nationalists.[10]

Yet, the KMT also seemed committed to significant reforms. First, a desire to gain popular support resulted in economic development policies which necessitated bringing technocrats into the top levels of what had been a military regime; and in the early 1960s the technocrats embarked upon a strategy of export-oriented growth that primarily benefitted the Islander entrepreneurs in the small business sector.[11] Second, the Chiang regime moved to coopt local political factions by instituting relatively free elections for local offices which allowed the central party organization to play off competing factions against each other. As time passed, however, elections became more important, thereby transferring power to the primarily Islander politicians who could draw votes at the polls.[12]

The processes set off by these two structural factors helped create several distinct segments of the middle class. The business community, for example, had interests and perspectives that would not necessarily be shared by the growing number of well-educated professionals and technicians, although both groups would be considered middle class. Intellectuals, moreover, would be expected to be much more critical and politicized, creating a third middle class group within Taiwan's "civil society." Finally, the KMT technocrats and electoral politicians can also be considered a segment of the middle class who possessed a considerable potential to become alienated from an authoritarian military regime. Indeed in the 1980s, the principal segments of the middle class formed a "tacit coalition" that pushed democratization -- that is, they favored political reform for somewhat different reasons and, while not necessarily cooperating or even agreeing with one another, acted to push the agenda for further democratization.[13]

Democracy in the Republic of China became institutionalized within a surprisingly short period of time -- approximately the half a decade between 1986 when an opposition party was formed in defiance of martial law to 1991 when the forced retirement of "senior legislators" (i.e. the large majorities of the Legislative Yuan and National Assembly who had been elected from Mainland constituencies in the late 1940s) established the electoral basis for democracy -- that is, that the people select their government in free and fair elections.[14] Furthermore, Taiwan's democracy has arguably reached the point of "consolidation," as particularly indicated by the drubbing that the KMT took in the 2000 presidential elections. That is, the reimposition of dictatorship (e.g., by a military coup) appears quite improbable.[15]

The ROC's "transition to democracy" probably began in 1986 when the informal opposition declaration that it had become a formal political party, the Democratic Progressive Party or DPP. While establishing a new party was illegal under the provisions of the then existing martial law, Chiang Ching-kuo forced the ruling Kuomintang to accept the DPP and, in so doing, made an implicit promise to democratize the polity. As outlined in Table 2.1, Taiwan's democratic transition itself can be roughly divided into three subperiods based on the type of events that were occurring. From 1986 through 1991, the major events primarily involved "removing authoritarian institutions." Most importantly, the government lifted the Emergency Decrees of the late 1940s which had placed limits on the Constitution; and the Council of Grand Justices (Taiwan's Supreme Court) issued a ruling forcing the retirement of all senior legislators at the end of 1991. As the events listed in Figure 2.2 indicate, this democratic transition was both "pushed" by opposition challenges, such as the formation of the DPP and the massive student demonstrations in the Spring of 1990, and "pulled" by liberalizing reforms taken by the ruling party-state.

The second subperiod from December 1991 through December 1994

Table 2.1 Major Events in ROC's Democratic Transition

Removing Authoritarian Institutions

Sept 1986:	DPP forms in defiance of martial law; Chiang Ching-kuo intervenes to prevent criminal prosecution
July 1987:	Emergency Decree undergirding martial law lifted
Jan 1988:	Restrictions on press and demonstrations liberalized
Jan 1988:	Chiang Ching-kuo dies; Lee Teng-hui becomes President
Jan 1989:	New Law on Civic Organizations
May 1990:	Massive demonstrations against National Assembly; Lee promises further political reforms
June 1990:	Council of Grand Justices rules that all "senior legislators" must retire by end of 1991
July 1990:	National Affairs Conference develops consensus on completing democratization
April 1991:	National Assembly terminates Temporary Provisions Effective During the Period of Communist Rebellion

Exercising Popular Sovereignty

Dec 1991:	First fullscale election for National Assembly
Dec 1992:	First fullscale election for Legislative Yuan
Dec 1994:	First popular election for Provincial Governor and Mayors of Taipei and Kaohsiung
March 1996:	First direct election of President; Lee wins re-election handily

Growing Political Competitiveness

Aug 1993:	New Party formed from KMT dissidents
Dec 1994:	DPP's Chen Shui-bian elected Taipei Mayor KMT Mainlander James Soong elected Provincial Governor
Dec 1995:	KMT majority in Legislative Yuan elections so thin that a near "hung parliament" results
March 1996:	KMT wins 55% of seats in National Assembly, but falls far short of extraordinary majority needed for Constitutional Amendments
Nov 1997:	DPP wins majority of city & county executives
March 2000:	DPP's Chen Shui-bian wins Presidency with 39% of vote in fierce three-way contest; KMT candidate a distant third at 23%

is labeled "exercising popular sovereignty" because it was marked by the first full direct elections for the Legislative Yuan, National Assembly, Provincial Governor, Mayors of Taipei and Kaohsiung, and (jumping a little out of time sequence) the President in March 1996. Each of these elections was precedent-setting in the sense the citizenry of the ROC directly selected leaders (perhaps the hallmark of democracy) for the first time. For the National Assembly and Legislative Yuan, popular sovereignty had been denied by the huge majority of "senior legislators" in each who were beyond the reach of the electorate. The provincial governor and the mayors of Taipei and Kaohsiung (Taiwan's two largest cities which were accorded provincial-level status) had been appointive positions; and the President had been indirectly elected by the National Assembly. Thus, giving the ROC's citizens the power to select these officials and to hold them accountable for their actions could be considered the core of Taiwan's democratization.

The third period includes the major events in the growing competitiveness of Taiwan's party system which ended the Kuomintang's *de facto* control over the government. The data on election results in Table 2.2, for example, demonstrate that 1986 clearly marked the beginning of a decided decline in the Kuomintang's domination of Taiwan's politics. Up through the mid-1980s, the KMT received two-thirds of the vote or more in most elections, while the opposition or *tangwai* (literally, those outside the party) averaged significantly under a fifth. The emergence of the DPP as a formal opposition party clearly cut into the electoral support of the ruling party. Still, the Kuomintang continued to dominate the polity as it bested the DPP by margins of approximately two-to-one during the late 1980s and early 1990s. The Democratic Progressive Party obviously was the major beneficiary when the New Party split off from the KMT in 1993. Yet, the DPP's popularity was clearly increasing as well as can be seen in the 1993 elections for city and county chief executives in which the KMT outpolled the DPP by only six percentage points (47% to 41%), despite the New Party's only receiving minimal support. Beginning with the 1992 elections for the Legislative Yuan, moreover, the Kuomintang could win only 45% - 55% of the vote, which certainly seemed to indicate that its days as the "ruling party" of the Republic of China were numbered.

Several elections stand out in the growing competitiveness of Taiwan's election. In 1994, the DPP's Chen Shui-bian won a hotly contested three-way race for Mayor of Taipei, while James Soong, a Mainlander KMT leader, handily won the race for Provincial Governor.

Table 2.2 Electoral Support of Major Parties

	KMT	DPP/ Tangwei	NP
1980 Legislative Yuan	72%	13%	--
1980 National Assembly	66%	--	--
1981 Magistrates/Mayors	57%	23%	--
1983 Legislative Yuan	69%	19%	--
1985 Magistrates/Mayors	61%	13%	--
1986 Legislative Yuan	67%	25%	--
1986 National Assembly	64%	24%	--
1989 Legislative Yuan	59%	29%	--
1989 Magistrates/Mayors	56%	30%	--
1991 National Assembly	71%	24%	--
1992 Legislative Yuan	53%	31%	--
1993 Magistrates/Mayors	47%	41%	3%
1994 Provincial Governor	56%	39%	4%
1995 Legislative Yuan	46%	33%	13%
1996 President	54%	21%	15%*
1996 National Assembly	50%	30%	14%
1997 Magistrates/Mayors	42%	43%	2%
1998 Legislative Yuan	46%	30%	7%
2000 Presidential	23%**	39%	1%

*Votes for Lin Yang-kang who was an Independent closely associated with the New Party.
**KMT defector James Soong, who ran as an Independent, received 37% of the vote.

Sources
Government Information Office. "The Tenth Presidential Election, Republic of China." www.elect2000.gov.tw.
Chih-cheng Lo. "Effects of the 1998 Elections," In Chien-min Chao and Cal Clark, Eds. *The ROC on the Threshold of the 21st Century: A Paradigm Reexamined*. Baltimore: School of Law, University of Maryland, 1999. p. 73.
Hung-mao Tien, Ed. *Taiwan's Electoral Politics and Democratic Transition:Riding the Third Wave*. Armonk, NY: M.E. Sharpe, 1996. pp. 16-17 & 109.

Together these outcomes suggest falling taboos that inhibited both the minority party and the minority ethnic group from gaining electoral success. Next, both the 1995 elections for the Legislative Yuan and the 1996 elections for the National Assembly produced KMT majorities that were too small to give the party effective control of these bodies. In the Legislative Yuan, the Kuomintang ended up with a razor-thin majority: 85 of 164 seats versus 54 for the DPP and 21 for the New Party. The KMT won a more solid majority of 55% of the National Assembly seats in 1996. However, since an extraordinary majority is needed to pass the constitutional amendments with which the National Assembly deals, this meant that the KMT needed significant support from opposition party members to do anything. The DPP won for the first time in the 1997 elections for the chief executives of counties and cities when it narrowly outpolled the KMT in the popular vote (43% to 42%) but won double the number of contests (12 to 6 with three victories by Independents). Finally, Chen's dramatic victory in the March 2000 presidential elections (and the smooth transition of administrations that followed in May) proved that full competition had been reached and that democracy in the Republic of China had clearly been consolidated.

Turning to the second perspective on democracy, specific agreements or "pacts" among the leading political parties and factions helped push the democratization process forward, in line with recent studies and theorizing which have concluded that such pacts are the key to most democratic transitions.[16] Table 2.3, therefore, outlines four such pacts among the leading political forces in Taiwan that were associated with the founding of the opposition Democratic Progressive Party (DPP) in 1986, the National Affairs Conference (NAC) in 1990, and the National Development Conference (NDC) in 1996. The first is generally considered to have marked the beginning of the democratic transition in the Republic of China. The second represented a critical step toward full democratization when the NAC reached a consensus among broad segments of the political elite including the opposition DPP on such controversial issues as the retirement of senior legislators that allowed President Lee and reformers within the KMT to overcome the opposition of the KMT old guard. The last two were agreements that were reached at the NDC concerning cross-Strait relations and constitutional reform. The former was a surprising all-party consensus on probably the most contentious issue in Taiwan politics, while the latter resulted from a KMT-DPP alliance against the New Party.

Table 2.3 Pacts in Taiwan's Political Development

EVENT	PACT	POLITICAL LOGIC	RESULTS
DPP FORMED "ILLEGALLY" IN 1986	Government does not react when new party declared in defiance of martial law	Chiang Ching-kuo forces KMT old guard to accept logic of democratization	Fairly rapid democratic transition commenced
NATIONAL AFFAIRS CONFERENCE	Consensus on final steps for democracy	Lee Teng-hui uses public forum to overcome opposition within KMT	Crosscutting cleavages on national identity, social welfare, and corruption ensure enough success and ambiguity in elections, so all parties support democracy
NATIONAL DEVELOPMENT CONFERENCE #1	Consensus on cross-Strait relations	Threat from PRC and voter support for status quo de-escalates issue	Space created for small parties with polar positions
NATIONAL DEVELOPMENT CONFERENCE #2	KMT-DPP agree on strengthening Presidency and downgrading Provincial Government	Shared interests of Lee & Hsu; ability to force party unity in NDC & NA shows pressures for two-party system	Juxtaposition with cross-Strait consensus indicates cross-cutting cleavages in polity

The first pact, which set off Taiwan's democratic transition in 1986, resulted when the government acquiesced to the formation of the Democratic Progressive Party in defiance of the martial law prohibition against new political parties. Following several months of inconclusive negotiations with the KMT over liberalizing the restrictions on "civic associations," the opposition then seemingly threw down the gauntlet to the regime when it declared the formation of the DPP on September 28. A political crisis appeared imminent as the Ministry of Justice filed charges against it for violating martial law restrictions, but President Chiang defused the situation by announcing that martial law would be ended and that new political parties could be formed as long as they supported the Constitution and renounced both communism and Taiwan Independence. The DPP then held a Congress in early November (despite renewed government warnings that it would be illegal) which adopted a party charter and program advocating "self-determination" and readmittance to the United Nations for Taiwan in vague enough language to stop just short of a direct challenge to the regime.[17]

Almost certainly, the key event that permitted the final steps of Taiwan's democratization to be taken was an "elite settlement" between the dominant faction of the ruling party and the opposition which was worked out at the National Affairs Conference (NAC) that President Lee Teng-hui called in the summer of 1990 in response to massive student demonstrations. The NAC brought together representatives of diverse parts of the country's political spectrum in an unprecedented forum that created the consensus necessary to break the gridlock over such issues as the retirement of the senior legislators that held back full democratization. Much to the surprise of many (if not most) observers the NAC turned out to be quite a success. The debate was spirited but serious (unlike the raucous battles in many of the island's legislative arenas); and the Conference produced a consensus upon how to move political reform in the ROC forward (in particular, by forcing the retirement of the "senior legislators") that was soon turned into official policy and constitutional change.[18]

The last two pacts were negotiated during the National Development Conference in December 1996 which President Lee called after his re-election in 1996 with the evident hope of replicating the NAC's ability to overcome political gridlock. One outcome of the NDC that would seem truly astounding was the consensus that was reached among the three major parties in the area of cross-Strait relations, despite the extreme divisiveness of this issue and its major salience within Taiwan. As will be discussed in more detail in the third section, all three parties seemingly reached the conclusion independently that de-escalating this issue was highly desirable. The other pact concerned constitutional reform. Here, Lee's faction in the KMT reached an agreement with DPP factions loyal to then party chair Hsu Hsin-liang to strengthen the powers of the Presidency vis-a-vis the Legislative Yuan and to downgrade the Provincial government drastically which was then forced through the NDC and later approved in somewhat modified form by the National Assembly despite strident opposition from the New Party and significant factions within both the KMT and DPP.[19]

The democratic development of the Republic of China, therefore, rests on a series of consensuses or "pacts" about how the political system should operate.[20]   These elite settlements involved somewhat differing political dynamics, though. In the first two cases (the formation of the DPP and the National Affairs Conference), Chiang Ching-kuo and Lee Teng-hui, respectively, expanded participation in decision-making from just the KMT to include broader forces in society, especially the political opposition, thereby tipping the balance against the veto which the KMT old guard tried to exercise over political change. The third (concerning cross-Strait relations) represented a broad all-party consensus to de-escalated the most divisive issue facing the country, while the fourth was much more the result of factional intrigue in which some elite groups agreed to tip the rules of the game in their favor at the expense of other elites.

The Challenges of Democratization

Several theoretical perspectives suggest that democratization may (but not necessarily will) create challenges for and instability in developing nations, such as the Republic of China on Taiwan. This section briefly sketches four of them and assesses their potential applicability to Taiwan, given the nature of democratization in the ROC as described in the previous section. Two of these approaches are derived from the central variables emphasized by the leading perspectives on democratic transition which (as noted at the beginning of the previous section) focus, respectively, upon modernization and the development of a strong middle class and upon "elite settlements" between authoritarian regimes and the leaders of opposition political movements. If either of these conditions are problematic, therefore, the relevant theoretical perspective predicts that new democracies may prove fragile and unstable. The third argues that the nature of certain issues is especially divisive and dangerous; so that the threat of democratization to social stability is determined by their presence or absence in a polity. Finally, another perspective looks to the distribution of public opinion on vital issues as the best predictor of the consequences of democratic competition.

Samuel Huntington's influential theory of the dangers of "political decay" constituted a very significant shift in how modernization theory viewed political development. Previously, democratic transitions in the Third World were seen as part of a fairly linear process of modernization and development that followed the "passing of traditional society." By the late 1960s, however, this optimistic perspective was sharply challenged by the failures of many new democracies in the Third World. Huntington argued that the very processes of democracy itself created the problem. New democracies might well have very little "capacity," either in terms of the resources that they controlled or the level of bureaucratic competence of their administrations. Yet, they faced huge demands from populations going through the traumas of early industrialization. The result was that such democratic governments often could not respond effectively to popular pressures, leading to chaos, governmental breakdown, and the re-imposition of authoritarian controls (e.g., by military coup). Consequently, Huntington and developmental scholars sympathetic to this theory began to place more emphasis on institutionalization, developing competent bureaucracies, and insulating governments from too much popular pressure than on democracy per se as the hallmark of political development.[21]

The situation surrounding the ROC's democratic transition suggests that the "Huntington problem" should not have emerged in any but the most muted form for two distinct reasons. First, democratization in Taiwan was delayed until quite late in the process of industrialization. Thus, a highly educated and prosperous middle class had developed which was not subject to the economic privation and fears that can lead to political demands that overwhelm a poor government. Second, the administration of the Republic of China had a well deserved reputation for competence dating back to the 1950s. In fact, its highly skilled technocrats were widely credited with leading the island's industrial transformation, that is, with solving economic and social problems rather than exacerbating them.[22]

The emphasis on elite settlements implies that the process of democratization itself provides a key to future political stability. If the leaders of both an authoritarian regime and the opposition to it can reach an explicit agreement or pact on the political rules of the game, democracy should be both legitimized and protected. Even if future disagreements arise about fundamental constitutional issues, the precedent of the initial settlement can send the contending parties back to the negotiating table to iron out their difficulties, rather than to the barricades or the barracks to start a civil war. Thus, democracies that are based on elite settlements should have a large advantage over those that are not in proceeding through successful democratic transitions without undue conflict or disruption.

Again, Taiwan's democratization as described in the preceding section would appear to be one that should have been in an excellent position to avoid civil strife and anti-democratic coups. The decade or so of democratic transition in the Republic of China commenced with a pact between the regime and the opposition that greatly strengthened democratic competition at the polls; and, subsequently, new elite settlements or pacts were used to push the process of democratization forward (see Table 2.3 above).[23] The only caveat that might be raised is that most of these "pacts" (all except the last one in Table 2.3 which itself reflected factional jockeying much more than democratic development) were "tacit" ones in the sense that they did not involve explicit agreements. This raised no problem with the first pact since the new Democratic Progressive Party was accepted as a legitimate participant in Taiwan's politics almost immediately. However, the National Affairs Conference was followed by bitter battles within the National Assembly over constitutional reform, demonstrating that a bipartisan consensus on this issue certainly did not exist;[24] and few (if any) analysts and observers of Taiwan's politics would be rash enough to argue that the consensus on cross-Strait relations that emerged from the National Development Conference took this issue off the ROC's political agenda. Even so, Taiwan's record on elite settlements shows that leaders can shelve their differences and agree on the basic "rules of the game" in the face of the periodic challenges to democratization that have risen.

The third approach focuses upon the nature of the most important political cleavages or issues within a society. Some issues, it is assumed, are much more polarizing and destabilizing than others. For much of the postwar period, class polarization between business and workers and between the rich and the poor was generally seen as the most divisive issue that could split polities apart. Where class conflict was muted and moderate, democratic politics could thrive; where it was highly polarized, instability and threats to democracy could easily arise. The institutional arrangements most able to dampen class conflict, in addition, appear to be "corporatist" ones in which government bargains with "peak associations" representing business and labor over economic and social policy.[25] More recently, such events as the implosion of Yugoslavia, the tragedy of genocide in Burundi and Rwanda, and separatism in many countries (e.g., Quebec in Canada) have turned scholarly attention to ethnic and nationalistic conflicts as presenting the gravest threat to democracy because of their deep-seated and highly emotional and symbolic nature which makes conflict resolution almost impossible.[26]

The situation in the ROC regarding these two issues was diametrically different.   Class conflict had never been particularly pronounced, in part because of the government's repressive policies toward labor. Yet, before democratization the Mainlander-dominated government did not have cordial relations with the primarily Islander business community.[27] Many thought that democratization would unleash the pent-up frustrations of labor, but this did not occur for a variety of reasons including Taiwan's high level of prosperity and the small-scale nature of much of the island's industry.   Conversely, there was no move toward corporatist bargaining among the government, business, and labor. Rather, class issues and cleavages remained surprisingly marginalized in Taiwan's politics.[28]

While class polarization remained a distant threat to Taiwan's nascent democracy, ethnic hostility and conflict were widely seen as much more probable.   The danger that democratization might prove counterproductive to effective government and social stability was probably most widely seen in the area of relations between Mainlanders and Islanders. The KMT's brutal military occupation of the island in the late 1940s and Mainlanders' domination of the top-level party and state positions through the death of Chiang Ching-kuo in 1988 created a significant amount of mutual hostility and suspicion. Thus, the very question of national identity (i.e., whether Taiwan's residents were Chinese or had a separate Taiwanese identity) had long smoldered under the surface of political discourse.

Throughout the years of authoritarian rule the Mainlanders legitimized the KMT regime by claiming that it was the government of all China; and, to maintain its advantage, the regime strictly enforced anti-sedition laws against advocating Taiwan Independence. Starting in the late 1980s, though, the expanding freedom of speech on the island finally allowed the national identity issue to be discussed, at first fairly covertly but then quite openly and stridently.[29] The danger that this presented was obvious. If the citizenry split over the fundamental question of "who are we?", the resulting ethnic polarization could threaten the new democratic institutions. On the one hand, a popular upswelling of repressed bitterness against the KMT regime could lead to a new round of repression to maintain public order. On the one hand, the victory of an Islander majority might prove short-lived. For example, the Mainlander-dominated conservative military might stage a coup against an Islander-dominated "Republic of Taiwan;" or the declaration of independence could spark military intervention from China to enforce its claims of sovereignty over Taiwan.[30]

Table 2.4 Effects of the Nature of Public Opinion Upon National Party Systems and Political Stability

Public Opinon	**Likely Impact on Party System**	**Implications for Political Stability**
Distribution of Public Opinion		
Normal or "Bell shaped"	Two catch-all parties	Stabilizing
Polarized or "Inverted U shaped"	Highly ideological parties	Destabilizing
Congruence of Issues		
Cross-cutting	Moderate catch-all parties	Stabilizing
Cumulative	Ideologically polarized parties	Destabilizing

The final approach focuses on the nature of public opinion within a society as the major determinant of whether democratization will set off destabilizing conflicts.   From this perspective, the nature of public opinion is assumed to shape the party system in a democratic polity which, in turn, can either exacerbate or attenuate political conflict in a society. As outlined in Table 2.4, this analytic focus concentrates upon two dimensions of public opinion. The first is the distribution of attitudes on the central issues of the day. When public opinion on most issues has a "normal" or "bell-shaped" distribution (i.e., most people hold moderate views near the middle of the ideological spectrum), large "catchall" parties should emerge because extremist parties will garner little support. Conversely, when public opinion is sharply polarized in an "inverted U-shaped" distribution, strong ideological divisions among conflictual parties should be expected. Second, the salient issues in a polity may be either "cross-cutting" (i.e., groups that agree on some issues disagree on others) or "cumulative" (i.e., the same groups or constituencies agree or disagree on most issues). The former situation should stimulate large catchall parties, while the latter often leads to a polarized party system.[31]

At the dawn of Taiwan's democracy, the nature of public opinion was something of a question mark. Critics of the regime argued that the populace was sharply polarized over ethnic or class issues and that only authoritarian political controls had preserved the image of stability. Supporters, on the other hand, believed that the Kuomintang's impressive victories at the polls reflected public opinion that gave the regime credit for Taiwan's rapid development and that feared radical change which could put the island's prosperity at risk. Which line of argument turned out to be correct, in turn, would probably determine the success and long-term stability of democracy in Taiwan.

This review of four theoretical predictions of potential problems in democratizing countries is somewhat ambiguous concerning the position of the Republic of China. As summarized in Table 2.5, Taiwan's position differed markedly on these potential threats to democratic stability. On the one hand, Taiwan's delayed democratization meant that it had a strong middle class and highly capable government administration which could serve as bulwarks against instability; and the prominent role of "elite settlements" in the ROC's process of democratization suggested a promising ability to work out disagreements over the "rules of the game." On the other hand, the fact that national identity was widely seen as the key issue and cleavage in Taiwan's politics suggested that the lifting of authoritarian controls over political discourse could lead to escalating conflict and confrontation which would be especially dangerous given the linkage

Table 2.5 Theoretical Dangers to Democracy and the Situation in Taiwan

Theory of Challenge to Democracy	Situation in Taiwan at Beginning of Democratic Transition
Political "decay" because government becomes overloaded with popular demands due to 1) the lack of development of a broad middle class and 2) the absence of a skilled administrative structure	Danger minimal because of large prosperous middle class and sophisticated administration
Democratization by "pacts" stabilizing both by defining political "rules of the game" and by setting precedent for negotiations between opposing political forces	Series of pacts, while mostly "tacit," suggest good prospects for democratic stability
Some issues, such as those involving class or ethnic polarization, much more destabilizing than others	Little evidence of class conflict in ROC, but centrality of "national identity" question posed potentially grave threat to democratizing polity
When attitudes on major issues have normal distributions and cross-cutting cleavages, politics should be stable and moderate; conversely, when the population is polarized on issues for which the sides are generally the same, instability and conflict is much more likely	The distribution of public opinion was the big question mark at the beginning of Taiwan's democratization, in particular whether the citizenry would polarize over the national identity issue

between the national identity issue and cross-Strait relations. How potent or real this danger was, in turn, seemingly depended upon the fourth variable included in Table 2.5, the nature of public opinion in the ROC. Only time could tell, of course, how this last factor would play out, but it clearly was key to the success of democracy in Taiwan and (given the potential threat from the People's Republic of China) perhaps even to the most fundamental security of the Republic of China.

Democracy as a (Perhaps) Suprising Force for Stability and Security in the ROC

The danger that democratization *potentially* represented for the national security of the Republic of China came from an easy to understand scenario. If the lifting of authoritarian controls resulted in strident clashes between Islanders and Mainlanders, this civil strife could destroy the new and fragile democracy. Moreover, this could reignite the security threat from the PRC that had lain dormant during the 1980s for either of two reasons that might provoke military intervention by he Chinese: 1) the breakdown of civil order in Taiwan; or 2) the assumption of power by an Islander-led political force, such as the Democratic Progressive Party, who was committed to proclaiming Taiwan Independence from China. If anything like this scenario were to occur, democracy would represent a challenge and threat to Taiwan's national security.

One can certainly adduce some historical evidence that is consistent with such a doleful scenario. Thus, this section begins by reviewing several sets of events that seem consistent with the argument that democratization has created problems for Taiwan's security by destabilizing cross-Strait relations. However, a closer examination of even this sequence indicates that it is not entirely consistent with the thesis that democratization in the ROC has worked to destabilize cross-Strait relations. Thus, the next subsection turns to the nature of public opinion on Taiwan and finds that it should attenuate, not exacerbate, political cleavages. Finally, based on this composition of public opinion, the third subsection presents a sequence of events suggesting that the dynamics of democratic politics have seemingly operated in such a manner as to defuse, not inflame, subethnic relations on Taiwan.

Evidence that Democratization Exacerbated the National Identity and National Identity Issues

Many expected that democratization would inflame the interlinked issues of national identity and cross-Strait relations. The first issue concerned the question of whether Taiwan's citizens were Chinese or Taiwanese; and the second concerned whether Taiwan's ultimate goal was to become part of a unified Chinese nation and state or to become an independent polity. These questions were not simply abstract or theoretical, but involved the basic issue of who should govern Taiwan. Up through the late 1980s, for example, the Kuomintang used the "one China" principle (i.e., that there is only one China and that Taiwan is part of it) to justify denying the current citizens of the ROC the right to elect their leaders in the national government. Conversely, the opposition *tangwai's* and then DPP's calls for democracy reflected the belief that the people of Taiwan should select their own leaders and determine their own fate, including (for some) the establishment of a "Republic of Taiwan" (although this last goal could not be openly proclaimed because of existing sedition laws).

Indeed, democratization brought a greatly increased emphasis upon the nationality issue in Taiwan; and several crises in cross-Strait relations erupted when China perceived that the ROC was moving too overtly toward Taiwan Independence. Figure 2.2 sketches these events which can be divided into three discrete stages. The first stage occurred during 1991-1993 when the salience of the national identity question jumped sharply and when a policy shift in response to public opinion clearly exacerbated relations between Taipei and Beijing. The feared degeneration into ethnic hostility seemed to be coming true in 1991 when the DPP's more radical New Tide faction forced the more reformist Formosa faction to include an explicit commitment to the goal of Taiwan Independence in the party's charter (in return for not creating their own party and for electing a party chair from the Formosa faction). Subsequently, national identity became a central issue in the 1991 campaign for National Assembly seats which was notable for its strident and conflictual tone.[32]

The national identity issue proved to be contentious within the ruling Kuomintang as well. When Chiang Ching-kuo died in January 1988, he was succeeded by his hand-picked Vice President, Dr. Lee Teng-hui, an Islander technocrat, both as President and (after significant factional struggle) as Chairman of the KMT. The party soon divided into pro-Lee and anti-Lee factions which came to be called the Mainstream and Anti-Mainstream factions. While this division reflected ideology and personal power considerations to some extent, the core of the Anti-Mainstream group was composed of older Mainlanders in top government, party, and military positions who put strong emphasis on the "one China" heritage of the ROC and were suspicious that President Lee might have ambitions to become the "father of his country" by covertly promoting Taiwan Independence.

The rise of Lee Teng-hui and the Mainstream faction within the KMT changed the image of the KMT dramatically. Previously, the KMT had been seen as a Mainlander dominated party (even though the large majority of its members and most of its "electoral politicians" were Islanders); and the KMT adhered strictly to a "One China" policy of Unification. Lee's victory led to a "Taiwanization" of the Kuomintang; and, in reaction, a group of primarily young Mainlander politicians defected from the KMT in 1993 to found the New Party, suggesting increased ethnic polarization internally. The Mainstream faction also moved toward a somewhat more ambiguous commitment to "one China" that ultimately provoked the PRC. In particular, following Lee's forcing the Anti-Mainstream leader Hau Pei-tsun to resign as Premier (with the tacit support of the DPP) in 1993, the KMT reversed its position and grabbed a popular DPP issue, Taiwan's readmittance to the United Nations. However, the PRC had the power to prevent the issue even being discussed at the 1993 session. Lee's obvious frustration then led many to suspect that Taiwan had cast the vote which cost Beijing the 2000 Summer Olympics (recently, Taiwan's then representative on the Olympic Committee said that Lee had instructed him to vote for Sydney but that he had voted for Beijing anyway). Despite this tension, though, there was little deterioration in cross-Strait relations tensions, though, as Stage 1 in Figure 2.2 ended.[33]

The stalemate at the UN clearly helped set off the Taiwan Strait crisis of 1995-96 (Stage 2 in Figure 2.2), though. Lee seemingly became increasingly frustrated by his lack of success of Taiwan's U.N. campaign and by his inability to make significant breakthroughs in upgrading the diplomatic status of the ROC. Thus, Taiwan focused its diplomatic efforts on gaining permission for President Lee to go the United States to visit his *alma mater* Cornell University. When both houses of Congress almost unanimously passed a resolution in support of a Lee visit, the Clinton administration reversed itself (after the State Department had assured the PRC that no change in policy would occur). Lee's visit itself seemed quite

Figure 2.2 Model of How Conflict Over National Identity Escalated, Thereby Creating Crises in Cross–Strait Relations and a Security Challenge for the ROC

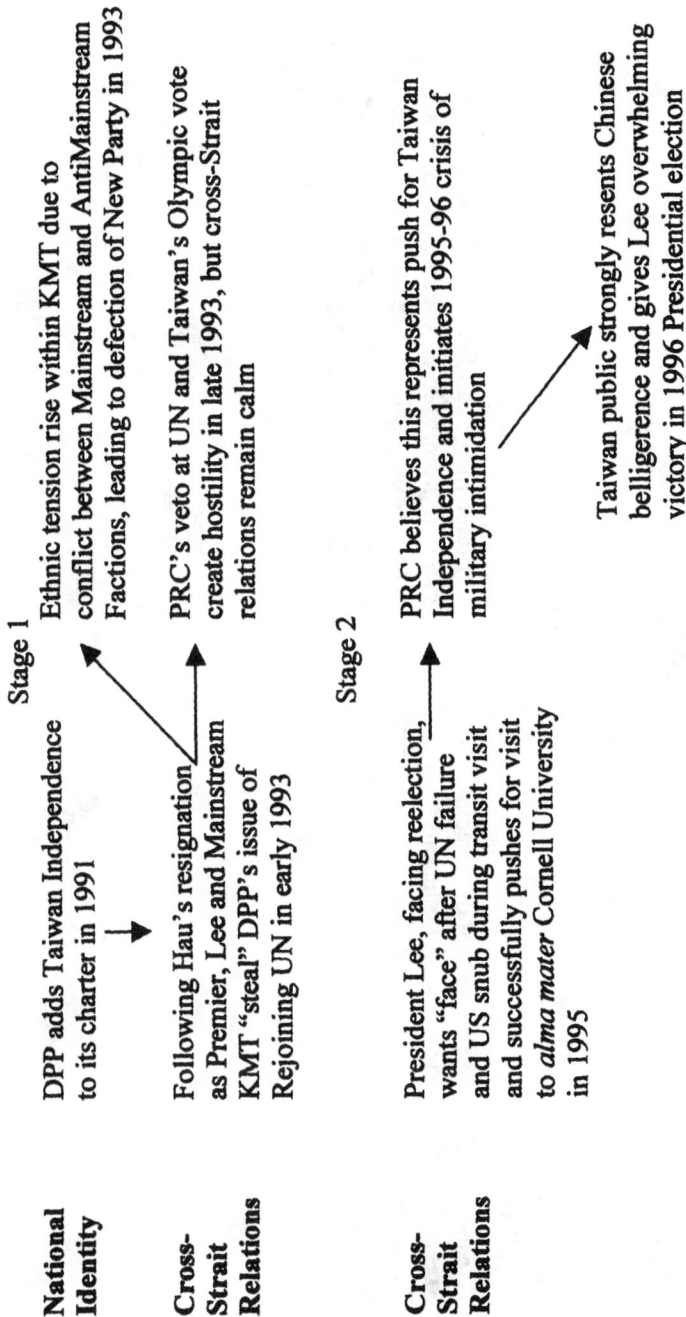

Stage 1

| National Identity | DPP adds Taiwan Independence to its charter in 1991 | | Ethnic tension rise within KMT due to conflict between Mainstream and AntiMainstream Factions, leading to defection of New Party in 1993 |

| Cross-Strait Relations | Following Hau's resignation as Premier, Lee and Mainstream KMT "steal" DPP's issue of Rejoining UN in early 1993 | | PRC's veto at UN and Taiwan's Olympic vote create hostility in late 1993, but cross-Strait relations remain calm |

Stage 2

| Cross-Strait Relations | President Lee, facing reelection, wants "face" after UN failure and US snub during transit visit and successfully pushes for visit to *alma mater* Cornell University in 1995 | | PRC believes this represents push for Taiwan Independence and initiates 1995-96 crisis of military intimidation |

Taiwan public strongly resents Chinese belligerence and gives Lee overwhelming victory in 1996 Presidential election

Figure 2.2 continued

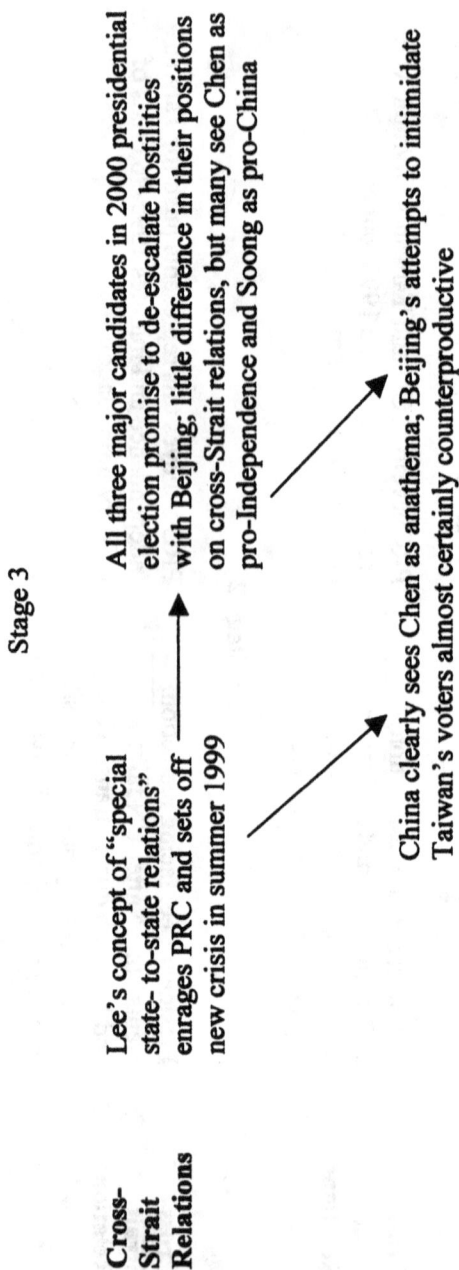

Stage 3

**Cross-
Strait
Relations**

Lee's concept of "special
state- to-state relations"
enrages PRC and sets off
new crisis in summer 1999

All three major candidates in 2000 presidential
election promise to de-escalate hostilities
with Beijing; little difference in their positions
on cross-Strait relations, but many see Chen as
pro-Independence and Soong as pro-China

China clearly sees Chen as anathema; Beijing's attempts to intimidate
Taiwan's voters almost certainly counterproductive

successful, but China went almost literally ballistic with a series of military tests and war games in 1995-1996 that were clearly aimed at intimidating Taiwan and influencing the March 1996 election. This pressure, if anything, added to Lee's popularity in Taiwan as he was seen as standing up for the country against Chinese bullying. Indeed, Lee was re-elected with resounding support; and both Taipei and Beijing appeared to agree tacitly to de-escalate their hostilities. Thus, this crisis can be explained fairly directly has democratization leading to a major change in Taiwan's policy which provoked the PRC, thereby creating a real threat to the island's national security.[34]

Stage 3 of cross-Strait interactions was, at least on the surface, almost a carbon copy of the 1995-96 contretemps. In July of 1999, President Lee, evidently fearful that the PRC was successfully marginalizing the ROC diplomatically (as evidenced by Clinton's declaration of the "Three No's" in Shanghai the previous year, for example), declared that "special state-to-state relations" existed between Taipei and Beijing. While Lee was careful to state that his concept simply represented a description of current reality, was not intended to change the nature of cross-State relations, and did not constitute a declaration of Taiwan Independence, Beijing responded with great hostility, setting off another Taiwan Strait crisis. Public opinion polls in Taiwan indicated that both President Lee and the concept of "special state-to-state relations" were extremely popular. This put cross-Strait relations high on the agenda for the upcoming 2000 elections with China viewing the DPP's nominee, Chen Shui-bian, as an advocate of Taiwan Independence whose election would force China to attack Taiwan to prevent the permanent separation of the island from the PRC. Even though Chen promised again and again not to declare Taiwan Independence and, indeed, differed little from the other major candidates in his position on cross-Strait relations, China continued to view him as anathema and almost went into shock when he won. Fortunately, Chen's "peace offensive" upon election appeared sufficient to mollify Beijing; and cross-Strait relations seemingly moved into a state of "cold peace."

At one level, therefore, the 2000 elections look like a replay of 1996 when democratic forces could be blamed for inflaming cross-Strait relations. Certainly, Lee's views on "special state-to-state relations" reflected public opinion; no candidate could afford to be seen as "soft" on the China threat (e.g., the supposedly pro-China presidential candidate, KMT maverick James Soong who was running as an Independent, issued the most out-spoken rebuffs to Chinese threats during the campaign); and the DPP's Chen, a one-time advocate of Taiwan Independence won the election. Yet, democracy itself does not really seem to have produced polarization on the national identity/cross-Strait relation issue. In fact, presumably responding to electoral dynamics, the major candidates differed little on cross-Strait relations; and the DPP's Chen was clearly more conciliatory toward Beijing than the incumbent KMT President Lee Teng-hui.[35] This certainly calls for a closer look at public opinion in the Republic of China.

Public Opinion in Taiwan: A "Moderate Middle" on National Identity and Cross-Strait Relations Plus Cross-Cutting Cleavages on Other Major Issues

The DPP's addition of a Taiwan Independence plank to their Charter in 1991 undoubted stemmed primarily from the desires of a leading group of party activists (what is termed the party's "core constituency" in the United States). It also reflected a bet on the nature of public opinion in Taiwan. That is, the call for Taiwan Independence would have been a political winner if most Islanders resented the long Mainlander domination of politics, identified as Taiwanese, and supported the creation of a Republic of Taiwan. Given the KMT's continuous strong support at the polls during the 1970s and 1980s (see Table 2.2), this might have appeared to be quite a long shot. Yet, the DPP could have anticipated that the end of authoritarian controls and intimidation might have freed the 85% Islander majority to express their true feelings. Thus, the DPP was betting that public opinion on the national identity and cross-Strait relations issues would polarize into an inverted U-shaped distribution with most Islanders identifying as Taiwanese and preferring Independence and most Mainlanders identifying as Chinese and preferring Unification. The huge majority of Islanders would then create a distribution that was highly skewed in the favor of the DPP.

Unfortunately for the DPP, this bet turned out to be a very poor one. It soon became clear that the citizens of the ROC possessed a very complex and multi-layered conception of national identity which combined both Chinese and Taiwanese elements. Table 2.6 presents fairly crude data from a 1995 survey (when Chinese military exercises should have, if anything, heightened Taiwanese nationalism) that asked whether respondents considered themselves Taiwanese, Chinese, or both. The results certainly indicate that public opinion on national identity was like a normal distribution in the sense that most of the public (51%) fell into the "moderate middle," although the "extreme" positions were somewhat unbalanced in the sense that there were significantly more Taiwanese identifiers (30%) than Chinese ones (19%). This complexity and ambiguity in how the citizens of the ROC feel about their national identity was reflected in the popularity of the concept of a "New Taiwanese" identity that is open to Islanders and Mainlanders alike:

> Taiwan's President Lee Teng-hui added drama to the Taipei mayoral campaign when he asked the KMT nominee, Ma Ying-jeou, "Where is your homeplace?" Ma, a Mainlander, replied in broken Minnan dialect, "I'm a New Taiwanese, eating Taiwanese rice and drinking Taiwanese water."[36]

Thus, in direct contrast to DPP expectations, the distribution of public opinion on national identity in Taiwan would have been expected to moderate, not exacerbate and polarize, political debate and policy-making. If the national identity issue did not follow DPP expectations, there was good reason to suspect that opinions on cross-Strait relations would not either. In fact, this 1995 poll found a similar distribution of public opinion on cross-Strait relations with most of the people in the "moderate middle" concerning the issue of what Taiwan's ultimate international status should be as 55% of the respondents preferred the current status quo of diplomatic limbo to either Independence or Unification. Moreover, Table 2.7 shows that this preference for the status quo in diplomatic status has remained quite constant throughout the 1990s and that a more detailed breakdown of the responses indicates an overwhelming degree of support for the status quo in the short-term ("don't know" probably can be considered an acceptance of the status quo by default). Clearly, the ROC's citizens (particularly the middle class who has the most to lose) fear that a premature commitment to *either* Independence or Reunification could destroy the social, economic, and political progress that Taiwan has already made. In addition, except for relatively small minorities (10% - 20% of the population) who are strongly committed to one alternative or the other, the island's citizens do not evidently see the future as a stark choice between these two alternatives. For example, a public opinion poll from August 1995 (just as the PRC was beginning its intimidation campaign), reported in Table 2.8 shows that both

Table 2.6 Public Opinion on National Identity and Cross-Strait Relations, 1995

	NUMBER	PERCENTAGE
Provincial Origin		
Taiwan	1,115	85%
Mainland	195	15%
National Identity		
Taiwanese	381	30%
Both	633	51%
Chinese	238	19%
Goal in Cross-Strait Relations		
Independence	183	16%
Status Quo	624	55%
Unification	337	29%

Post-election Survey of 1995 Legislative Yuan Election conducted by the Election Study Center of National Chengchi University.

Source
Teh-fu Huang and Ching-hsin Yu. "Developing a Party System and Democratic Consolidation." In Steve Tsang and Hung-mao Tien, Eds. *Democratization in Taiwan: Implications for China*. New York: St. Martin's 1999. p. 97.

Table 2.7 Attitudes in 1990s Toward Ultimate Goal for Cross-Strait Relations

	1991	1995	1998
Independence	3%	14%	20%
Status Quo	43%	46%	46%
Unification	27%	20%	16%
No Opinion	26%	20%	18%

	1998
Independence immediately	7%
Status quo now, Independence later	13%
Status quo indefinitely	15%
Status quo now, Decide later	31%
Unification immediately	1%
Status quo now, Unification later	15%
Don't know	18%

Sources

Shelly Rigger. "Is Taiwan Independence *Passe*? Public Opinion, Party Platforms, and National Identity in Taiwan." In Chien-min Chao and Cal Clark, Eds. *Th ROC on the Threshold of the 21ª Century: A Paradigm Reexamined*. Baltimore: School of Law's Series in Contemporary Asian Studies, 1999. p. 57.

Vincent Wei-cheng Wang. "Bill Clinton's 'Three No's' and Taiwan's Future." In Winston L. Yang and Deborah A. Brown, Eds. *Across the Taiwan Strait: Exchanges, Conflicts, and Negotiations*. New York: Center for Asian Studies, St. John's University, 1999. p. 299.

Unification or Independence were acceptable by approximately two-to-one margins if the change in status could be achieved without the dangers now associated with it (subordination to a communist dictatorship for Reunification and Chinese retaliation for Independence). In short, the fears that democratization would inflame Taiwanese nationalism proved to be far off the mark because the ROC's citizenry has moved to what Shelley Rigger terms a "post-nationalist" consciousness.[37]

The "bad bet" of the Democratic Progressive Party on the national identity and cross-Strait relations issues meant that a large proportion of the population almost certainly felt that it was too radical to be entrusted with power. Such anti-DPP feelings by themselves could have polarized the polity by marginalizing the DPP and making it increasingly frustrated, alienated, and radical as it hopes for winning power were crushed in election after election. However, this untoward result did not occur. Rather, the major players in Taiwan's political arena accepted the democratic rules of the game with surprising speed for a country with no history or tradition of democracy.

According to Yun-han Chu and Tse-min Lin, this ready acceptance of democracy occurred because of cross-cutting cleavages that allowed each of the major parties to have a broad enough appeal to be at least moderately successful at the polls. This success, in turn, encouraged them to concentrate their efforts on electoral politics rather than anti-system protests and activities.[38] In particular, as summarized in Table 2.9, the Kuomintang's advantages on the national identity issue and on being given credit for a successful development strategy were counterbalanced by support for the DPP's proposals to mitigate the side effects of rapid industrialization in the areas of the environment and social welfare policy and by their being by far the most tainted by the corruption of "black and gold" politics, which benefitted first the New Party and then the DPP. In addition, while KMT reformers probably garnered the most support for Taiwan's successful democratic transition, the DPP gained considerable credit as well. For example, in the 1980s and early 1990s, more than a few KMT members voted for DPP candidates in order to pressure the regime to speed up its political reforms.

A consideration of the nature of public opinion in the Republic of China, therefore, indicates that democratization should have produced moderate, rather than polarized, politics. On both the key issues concerning national identity and cross-Strait relations, most of the public evinced beliefs in the "moderate middle" rather than at the ideological extremes. Furthermore, the major issues in Taiwan were cross-cutting, not cumulative, in the sense that different parties represented majority opinion on different issues. As illustrated in Table 2.8, these characteristics of public opinion should push democratic politics in the direction of stability and moderation.

This certainly suggests that we should look again at Taiwan's politics during the 1990s in search of a pattern in which democracy in the ROC attenuated, not exacerbated, cross-Strait relations, thereby helping to *enhance* the national security of the Republic of China on Taiwan.

Table 2.8 Public Opinion on a Changed International Status for Taiwan, August 1995

	YES	NO
Unification with a Democratic and Prosperous China	54%	22%
New Taiwan Nation Peacefully Coexisting with PRC	47%	29%

Source: Tun-jen Cheng. "Taiwan in 1996: From Euphoria to Melodrama." *Asian Survey* 37 (1997) pp. 44-45.

How Democracy in Taiwan Stabilizes Cross-Strait Relations, Thereby Enhancing the ROC's National Security

Indeed, as diagramed in Figure 2.3, the impact of public opinion on Taiwan's electoral politics during the 1990s did seemingly act to moderate the divisiveness of the national identity and cross-Straits relations issues for two interconnected reasons. First, the nature of the KMT's leadership changed in a very significant way in the early 1990s that made a KMT-DPP battle over national identity obsolete. Second, espousal of either extreme position on national identity soon turned out to be counterproductive at the polls. Thus, increasingly over time, the dynamics of democracy itself undercut the polarizing potential of these issues.

The victory of President Lee Teng-hui and the Mainstream faction within the Kuomintang produced the "Taiwanization" of the party -- which made it hard to blame it for the repression and "white terror" of the "old Mainlander" Kuomintang. Moreover, Lee managed to straddle the national identity issue quite astutely in the early 1990s, implicitly portraying himself as a moderate between the pro-Independence DPP and pro-Unification Anti-Mainstream KMT and (after it split off from the KMT in 1993) New Party. Consequently, Lee's successful "Taiwanization" of the Kuomintang blurred its image considerably on the national identity question, while the DPP and New Party became associated with the two extreme alternatives.[39]

Table 2.9 Party Positions on Major Issues in Taiwan

	Late 1980s	Early 1990s	Late 1990s
National Identity & Ethnic Justice	Growing DPP challenge to KMT "one China" policy, but KMT largely preferred because of perceived DPP radicalism	Polarization between proIndependence DPP & proUnification KMT evolves when Pres. Lee & Mainstream KMT take "middle" stance	Growing cross-party consensus on "New Taiwanese" identity & status quo in cross-Strait relations; little advantage to any party
Democracy	KMT old guard trying to hold back reforms pushed by DPP and KMT reformers	Largely achieved	KMT begins to suffer from image of "party of past"
Black & Gold Politics	Fairly marginal on political agenda	KMT seen as most tainted, New Party as cleanest	Difference among parties narrow, but Soong scandal gives issue to DPP
Social Welfare Policy	Specific issues pushed by social movements	DPP takes lead in pushing for expansion of welfare state	KMT coopts popular DPP policies; now little difference among parties
Economic Development	KMT credited for ROC's prosperity	Still some advantage to KMT, but decreasing	Largely moot
Environment	DPP seen as pro-environmental party	DPP seen as pro-environmental party	DPP seen as pro-environmental party

Beyond, the radical change in the nature of the Kuomintang, the destabilizing effects of the national identity issue were offset because, in reality, it was a loser at the polls. Thus, while the DPP and NP got the strongest emotional response from their ostensibly core constituencies by making appeals to, respectively, Independence and Unification, such campaign strategies were probably counterproductive. Table 2.2 showed that the DPP's electoral support dropped by almost a third when it became too closely associated with advocacy of Taiwan Independence, as it did in the 1991 National Assembly and 1996 Presidential elections. The 1994 elections provide another good illustration of the political benefits of taking a moderate stance on national identity. In the race for Provincial Governor, James Soong, a Mainlander Mainstream KMT official who had not held elective office before, trounced an Islander DPP advocate of Taiwan Independence, while Chen Shui-bian won the mayorship of Taipei for the DPP handily by stressing a pragmatic and reformist agenda (contrary to his image of supporting Taiwanese nationalism).

These trends came together to moderate the differences among the parties dramatically on national identity and cross-Strait relations. For example, one outcome of the 1996 National Development Conference which would seem truly astounding was the three-party consensus that emerged in the area of cross-Strait relations, given the extreme divisiveness of this issue and its major salience within Taiwan. What evidently occurred was that the Chinese attempt at military intimidation in 1995-96 brought home the point that "politics ends at the water's edge." For the New Party and remnants of the KMT old guard, the popular antagonism that Chinese militarism aroused precluded advocating Unification except as a very long-term objective. For the DPP, the battering that their presidential candidate took at the polls for his pro-Independence stance suggested that association with Taiwan Independence was just as hazardous for a politician's or party's viability. Consequently, the agreed upon positions concerning cross-Strait relations generally reflected support for President Lee Teng-hui's "pragmatic diplomacy" of regarding Taiwan as a sovereign state and of aggressively seeking to upgrade Taiwan's international status, while paying verbal allegiance to the "one China" principle and to Unification as a goal for the indefinite future. Even when the New Party walked out of the NDP in protest over the majority's decisions concerning constitutional change, it indicated that it would support the consensus on cross-Strait relations.[40]

Figure 2.3 How Democratization Moderated the National Identity and Cross-Strait Relations and Cleavages

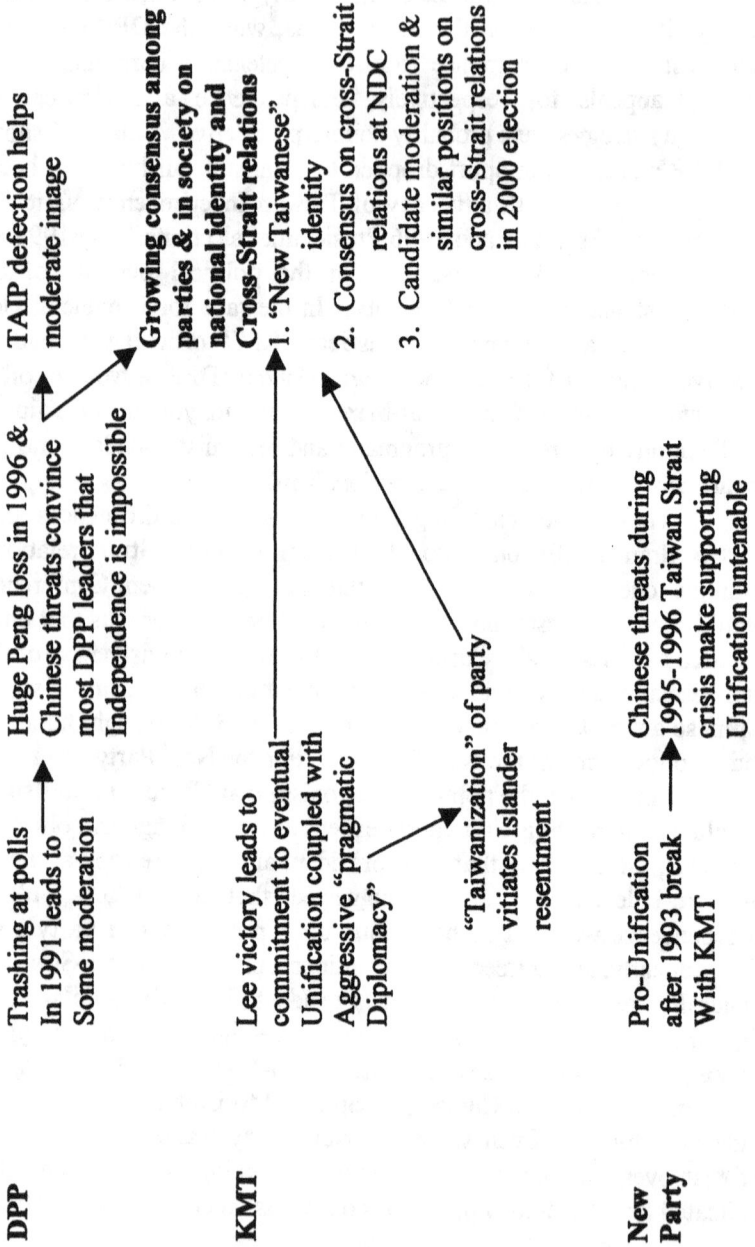

DPP

Trashing at polls In 1991 leads to Some moderation → Huge Peng loss in 1996 & Chinese threats convince most DPP leaders that Independence is impossible

TAIP defection helps moderate image

→ **Growing consensus among parties & in society on national identity and Cross-Strait relations**

1. "New Taiwanese" identity
2. Consensus on cross-Strait relations at NDC
3. Candidate moderation & similar positions on cross-Strait relations in 2000 election

KMT

Lee victory leads to commitment to eventual Unification coupled with Aggressive "pragmatic Diplomacy" → "Taiwanization" of party vitiates Islander resentment

New Party

Pro-Unification after 1993 break With KMT → Chinese threats during 1995-1996 Taiwan Strait crisis make supporting Unification untenable

The growing moderation and consensus in the debate over cross-Strait relations can also be seen in the 2000 presidential campaign. President Lee certainly tossed an extremely "hot potato" into the middle of the presidential campaign in July 1999 when his proposal of the theory of "special state-to-state relations" with Beijing enraged the Chinese and set off another crisis in the Taiwan Strait. Ironically, though, the way in which Lee presented the issue made it hard, if not impossible, for it to have much play in domestic politics. Lien Chan, who owed his nomination by the KMT to Lee's support, of course was constrained to support Lee's approach, even though he seemingly signaled that he would be significantly more accommodating toward the PRC. James Soong, who was widely perceived as the most favorable of the major candidates toward China, was deterred from criticizing Lee or even bringing up cross-Strait relations by the unpopularity of his "soft approach." Conversely, Chen Shui-bian and the DPP had been moving over the previous year or so to downplay their image as pro-Taiwan Independence (e.g., by explicitly accepting "Republic of China" as Taiwan's official name, which the DPP had never previously acknowledged). Consequently, Lee's "special state-to-state relations" theory, if anything, went beyond the DPP's position and made it hard (if not impossible) for them to advocate a more "hard line" position. Thus, while the candidates certainly criticized each other (and especially caricatures of the others) on cross-Strait relations, they all really articulated moderate positions of toning down hostilities with Beijing while not sacrificing Taiwan's existing autonomy and sovereignty that differed from one another much more in phraseology than substance.[41]

A second, more indirect dynamic linking democratization to moderation on cross-Strait relations was set off by the rapidly growing interdependence between Taiwan and southern coastal China in the early and mid1990s which meant that the increasingly powerful business sector gained a tremendous incentive to promote amity in relations between Beijing and Taipei. Economic interactions between Taiwan and the Mainland took off in the late 1980s after Taiwan liberalized its policy on cross-Strait contacts at precisely the time that Taiwan's economy was undergoing a fundamental transformation as the island's prosperity was pricing it out of low-wage manufacturing.

Many of Taiwan's businesses began to move labor-intensive parts of production "off shore" in the late 1980s; and the Chinese Mainland quickly became a prime location for new factory sites. The Chinese Mainland appeared a very enticing target for their commercial expansion for several important reasons. China has unlimited low-cost labor; language and cultural ties are very strong; and pragmatic provincial leaders offered substantial incentives to invest in export industries. In fact, by the early 1990s, there even appeared to be something of a movement toward economic integration between Taiwan and southern coastal China, especially Fujian Province which many Taiwanese "Islanders" (who dominate Taiwan's small business sector) regard as their ancestral home because Taiwanese investment produced much of the trade across the Taiwan Strait as the new factories of Taiwan's businesses on the Mainland imported machinery and more sophisticated components from Taiwan for the production of goods being exported to third markets (particularly the United States). Moreover, by the mid-1990s the nature of Taiwan investment in the PRC began to shift from small business in labor- intensive exports to much larger businesses seeking to penetrate the Chinese market in heavy industry (e.g., Formosa Plastics) and consumer goods (e.g., President Enterprises). Thus, the nature of the integration between the island and Mainland economies appears to be deepening to a very considerable extent.[42]

Figure 2.4 presents a more generalized model of how this growing economic integration acts to attenuate the diplomatic confrontation between Taipei and Beijing. In Taiwan, business pressure on the government to keep a lid on hostilities with China has been considerable; and its effectiveness has increased as more and more big businesses see major investment opportunities on the Mainland. For example, in the late 1990s, several important business leaders -- such as Kao Ching-yuan of President Enterprises (a member of the KMT's Central Standing Committee), Chang Rong-fa of Evergreen, and Y.C. Wang of Formosa Plastics -- openly dissented from the "Go Slow" policy toward cross-Strait economic relations. The pressure on Beijing is somewhat more indirect but none the less real for two interconnected reasons. First, China derives significant benefits from the large investment that it has received from Taiwan. Second, disrupting these economic interactions could shatter any vestiges of a movement toward "Greater China" that is gradually creating more and more linkages between the Mainland and Taiwan.[43]

Overall, therefore, the democratic processes in Taiwan appear to be working to dampen conflict with Beijing. Obviously, though, the two Taiwan Strait crises in the late 1990s indicate that   cross-Strait relations have become anything but calm. Three reasons may be adduced to explain

Figure 2.4 Political Pressures for Cross–Strait Amity Set Off by Growing Economic Integration Between Taiwan and Southern Coastal China

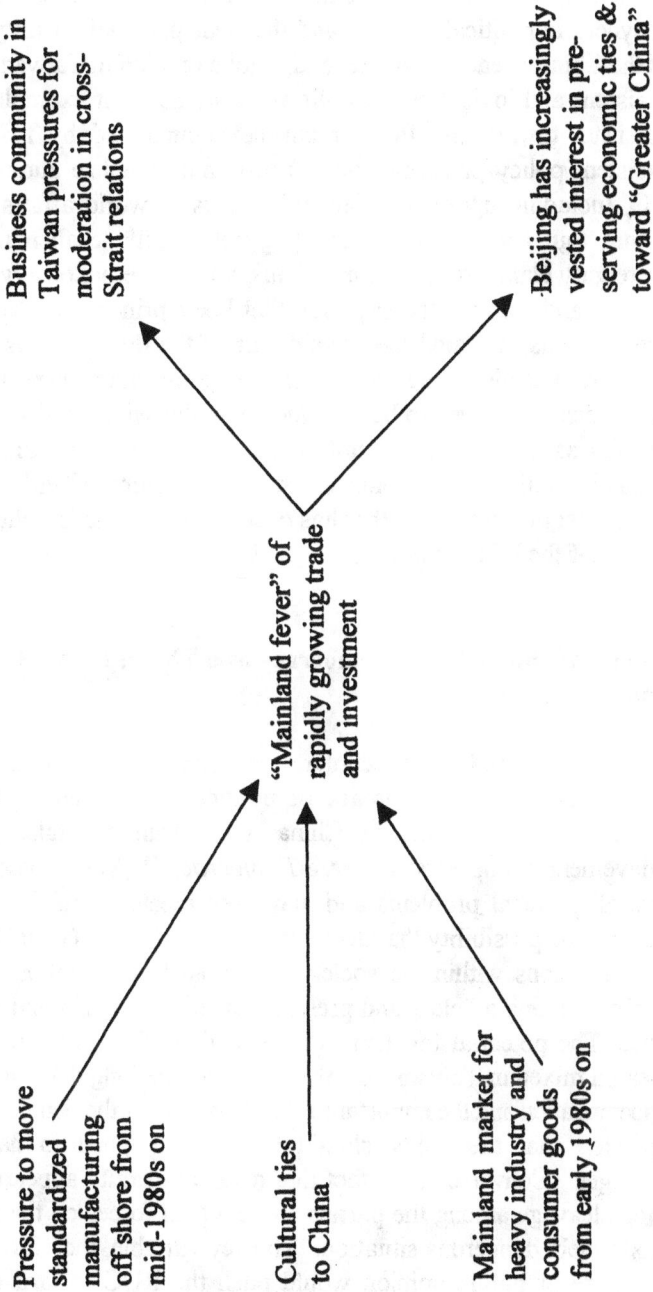

Business community in Taiwan pressures for moderation in cross-Strait relations

Beijing has increasingly vested interest in pre-serving economic ties & toward "Greater China"

"Mainland fever" of rapidly growing trade and investment

Pressure to move standardized manufacturing off shore from mid-1980s on

Cultural ties to China

Mainland market for heavy industry and consumer goods from early 1980s on this incongruity. The first relates to President Lee Teng-hui's somewhat idiosyncratic political strategy and the clear personal hostility between Lee and the Chinese leadership. Second, public opinion in Taiwan is not entirely consistent and logical on cross-Strait relations. For example, the public's consensus toward the PRC might be summarized by two not entirely consistent policy prescriptions: 1) maintain complete autonomy from the PRC, including upgrading Taiwan's status in world affairs and 2) avoid picking fights with China, including not directly challenging the PRC's sovereignty claims over Taiwan. Thus, while external observers, especially the PRC and many in the U.S., felt that Lee's principle of "special state-to-state relations" violated the second half of the dictum "preserve Taiwan's autonomy but don't needlessly challenge or antagonize China," Lee's pronouncement proved to be extremely popular with the Taiwan public who saw him as standing up to unfair Chinese aggression. Finally, the PRC seemingly failed to recognize, at least before Chen's election, the fundamental transformation that has occurred in Taiwan's politics (especially in terms of the DPP's views).

A Dog that Didn't Bark: Democracy as a Threat to the National Security of Taiwan

Many peoples and most scholars see democracy as desirable form of government and as a hallmark of political development. Certainly, the citizens of the Republic of China on Taiwan can take pride in their achievement as the *First Chinese Democracy*.[44] Yet, democracy does not solve all political problems and may even create them. This chapter has examined the possibility that democratization in Taiwan could have inflamed ethnic relations within the society and cross-Strait relations with Beijing, thereby creating a "clear and present danger" to the national security of the ROC. The potential for democracy's setting off counterproductive trends appeared mixed in Taiwan. On the one hand, the long delay in the country's democratization and the important role of "pacts" in the democratic transition suggested that the polity should be well equipped to handle political challenges. Conversely, the fact that national identity appeared to form the major cleavage among the parties and political forces on the island implied an extremely dangerous situation. The key variable, therefore, was whether the nature of public opinion would push the ROC toward moderation or polarization on the interconnected issues of national identity and cross-Strait relations. Fortunately, this factor turned out to work in the favor of stability and moderation. In fact, while the evidence is not entirely unambiguous, a sequence of moderating political change can be discerned. In short, Taiwan's democracy has functioned well in an area where significant fears existed at the beginning of the democratic transition.

Notes

1.   Edward Friedman, Ed., *The Politics of Democratization: Generalizing East Asian Experiences* (Boulder, CO: Westview, 1994); James A. Robinson, 1995. "Multiparty Democratic Values can also be Asian Values," *Free China Review* 45 (1995) pp. 36-42.

2.   Robert W. Jackman, *Politics and Social Equality: A Comparative Analysis* (New York: John Wiley, 1975); Seymour Martin Lipset, "Some Social Requisites of Democracy: Economic Development and Political Legitimacy," *American Political Science Review* 53 (1959) pp. 69-105.

3.   Gretchen Casper and Michelle M. Taylor, *Negotiating Democracy: Transitions from Authoritarian Rule* (Pittsburgh: University of Pittsburgh Press, 1996); Samuel P. Huntington, *The Third Wave: Democratization in the Late Twentieth Century* (Norman: University of Oklahoma Press, 1991); Guillermo O'Donnell, Philippe C. Schmitter, and Laurence Whitehead, Eds., *Transitions from Authoritarian Rule: Prospects for Democracy* (Baltimore: Johns Hopkins University Press, 1986).

4.   Linda Chao and Ramon H. Myers, *The First Chinese Democracy: Political Life the Republic of China* (Baltimore: Johns Hopkins University Press, 1998); Yun-han Chu, *Crafting Democracy in Taiwan* (Taipei: Institute for International Policy Research, 1992); John Higley, Tong-yi Huang, and Tse-min Lin, "Elite Settlements in Taiwan," *Journal of Democracy* 9:2 (1998) pp. 148-163; Steven J. Hood, *The Kuomintang and the Democratization of Taiwan* (Boulder, CO: Westview, 1997); Peter R. Moody, Jr., *Political Change on Taiwan: A Study of Ruling Party Adaptability* (New York: Praeger, 1992); Shelley Rigger, *Politics in Taiwan: Voting for Democracy* (London: Routledge, 1999); Hung-mao Tien, *The Great Transition: Political and Social Change in the Republic of China* (Stanford: Hoover Institution Press, 1989); Jaushieh Joseph Wu, *Taiwan's Democratization: Forces Behind the New Momentum* (Hong Kong: Oxford University Press, 1995).

5.   Susan Greenhalgh, "Families and Networks in Taiwan's Economic Development," pp. 224-245 in Edwin A. Winckler and Susan Greenhalgh, Eds., *Contending Approaches to the Political Economy of Taiwan* (Armonk, NY: M.E. Sharpe, 1988); Danny K.K. Lam and Ian Lee, "Guerrilla Capitalism and the Limits of Statist Theory," pp. 107-124 in Cal Clark and Steve Chan, Eds., *The Evolving Pacific Basin in the Global Political Economy: Domestic and International Linkages* (Boulder, CO: Lynne Rienner, 1992); Ian Skoggard, *The Indigenous Dynamic in Taiwan's Postwar Development: The Religious and Historical Roots of*

Entrepreneurship (Armonk, NY: M.E. Sharpe, 1996).

6.   Cal Clark, *Taiwan's Development: Implications for Contending Political Economy Paradigms* (New York: Greenwood, 1989); Walter Galenson, Ed., *Economic Growth and Structural Change in Taiwan: The Postwar Experience of the Republic of China* (Ithaca: Cornell University Press, 1979); Stephan Haggard, *Pathways from the Periphery: The Politics of Growth in the Newly Industrializing Countries* (Ithaca: Cornell University Press, 1990); Samuel P.S. Ho, *Economic Development in Taiwan, 1860-1970* (New Haven: Yale University Press, 1978); Ching-yuan Lin, *Industrialization in Taiwan, 1946-1972: Trade and Import Substitution Policies for Developing Countries* (New York: Praeger, 1973); Ramon H. Myers, "The Economic Transformation of the Republic of China on Taiwan," *China Quarterly* 99 (1984) pp. 500-528; Gustav Ranis, Ed., *Taiwan: From Developing to Mature Economy* (Boulder, CO: Westview, 1992); Wen-hui Tsai, *In Making China Modernized: Modernization between Mainland China and Taiwan* (Baltimore: University of Maryland School of Law, Series in Contemporary Asia Studies, 1993); Robert Wade, *Governing the Market: Economic Theory and the Role of Government in East Asian Industrialization* (Princeton: Princeton University Press, 1990); Edwin A. Winckler and Susan Greenhalgh, Eds., *Contending Approaches to the Political Economy of Taiwan* (Armonk, NY: M.E. Sharpe, 1988).

7.   Steve Chan and Cal Clark, *Flexibility, Foresight, and Fortuna in Taiwan's Development: Navigating between Scylla and Charybdis* (London: Routledge, 1992); Chao and Myers, *First Chinese Democracy*; Hood, *Kuomintang*; Tse-kang Leng, *The Taiwan-China Connection: Democracy and Development Across the Taiwan Straits* (Boulder, CO: Westview, 1996); Moody, *Political Change*; Rigger, *Voting for Democracy*; Hung-mao Tien, Ed., *Taiwan's Electoral Politics and Democratic Transition: Riding the Third Wave* (Armonk, NY: M.E. Sharpe, 1996); Winckler and Greenhalgh, *Contending Approaches*; Wu, *Taiwan's Democratization*.

8.   Tun-jen Cheng, "Taiwan in 1996: From Euphoria to Melodrama," *Asian Survey* 37 (1997) pp. 43-51; Cal Clark, "The 2000 Taiwan Presidential Elections," *Asia Update* (New York: The Asia Society, 2000); Hungmao Tien, "Taiwan in 1995: Electoral Politics and Cross-Strait Relations," *Asian Survey* 36 (1996) pp. 33-40.

9.   Clark, *Taiwan's Development*; Rigger, *Voting for Democracy*.

10.   Thomas B. Gold, *State and Society in the Taiwan Miracle* (Armonk, NY: M. E. Sharpe, 1986); Alam M. Wachman, *Taiwan: National Identity and Democratization* (Armonk, NY: M.E. Sharpe, 1994).

11.   Chan and Clark, *Flexibility, Foresight, and Fortuna*; Wade, *Governing the Market*.

12.   Joseph Bosco, "Taiwan Factions: *Guanxi*, Patronage and the State in Local Politics," pp. 114-144 in Murray A. Rubinstein, Ed., *The Other Taiwan: 1945 to Present* (Armonk, NY: M.E. Sharp, 1994); Ming-tong Chen, "Local Factions and Elections in Taiwan's Democratization," pp. 174-192 in Hung-mao Tien, Ed., *Taiwan's Electoral Politics and Democratic Transition: Riding the Third Wave* (Armonk, NY: M. E. Sharpe, 1994); Rigger, *Voting for Democracy*; Fang Wang, "The Political Economy of Authoritarian Clientelism in Taiwan," pp. 181-206 in Luis Roniger and Ayse Gunes-Ayata, Eds., *Democracy, Clientelism, and Civil Society* (Boulder, CO: Lynne Rienner, 1994).

13.   Chao and Myers, *First Chinese Democracy*; Chan and Clark, *Flexibility, Foresight,*

and Fortuna; Gold, *Taiwan Miracle*; Hsin-huang Michael Hsiao, "The Changing State-Society Relations in the ROC: Economic Change, the Transformation of Class Structure, and the Rise of Social Movements," pp. 127-140 in Ramon H. Myers, Ed., *Two Societies in Opposition: The Republic of China and the People's Republic of China After Forty Years* (Stanford: Hoover Institution Press, 1991); Tsai, *Making China Modernized*; Winckler and Greenhalgh, *Contending Approaches*.

14. Chao and Myers, *First Chinese Democracy*; John F. Copper, *A Quiet Revolution: Political Development in the Republic of China* (Washington, D.C.: Ethics and Public Policy Center, 1988); John F. Copper, *The Taiwan Political Miracle: Essays on Political Development, Elections and Foreign Relations* (New York: University Press of America, 1997); Moody, *Political Change*; Tien, *Great Transition*; Tien, *Taiwan's Electoral Politics*; Wu, *Taiwan's Democratization*.

15. See Huntington, *The Third Wave*, for the distinction between periods of "democratic transition" and "democratic consolidation."

16. Casper and Taylor, *Negotiating Democracy*; O'Donnell, et al., *Transitions*.

17. Copper, *Quiet Revolution*; Tien, *Great Transition*.

18. Chao and Myers, *First Chinese Democracy*; Chu, *Crafting Democracy*; Higley, et al., "Elite Settlements;" Hood, *Kuomintang*; Moody, *Political Change*; Wu, *Taiwan's Democratization*.

19. Cheng, "Taiwan in 1996;" Higley, et al., "Elite Settlements;" James A. Robinson, "Consensus Forged" *Free China Review* 47 (1997) pp. 30-32.

20. Higley, et al., "Elite Settlements."

21. Samuel P. Huntington, *Political Order in Changing Societies* (New Haven: Yale University Press, 1968).

22. Cal Clark, "Democracy, Bureaucracy, and State Capacity in Taiwan," *International Journal of Public Administration* 23 (2000) pp. 1833-1853 discusses this in much more detail.

23. Higley, et al., "Elite Settlements."

24. Chao and Myers, *First Chinese Democracy*; Copper, *Quiet Revolution*; Copper, *Taiwan Political Miracle*; Moody, *Political Change*; Tien, *Great Transition*; Tien, *Taiwan's Electoral Politics*; Wu, *Taiwan's Democratization*.

25. Philippe C. Schmitter and Gerhard Lehmbruch, Eds., *Trends in Corporatist Intermediation* (Beverly Hills, CA: Sage, 1979); Howard J. Wiarda, *Corporatism and Comparative Politics: The Other Great "Ism."* (Armonk, NY: M.E. Sharpe, 1997); Peter J. Katzenstein, *Small States in World Markets: Industrial Power in Europe* (Ithaca: Cornell University Press, 1985).

26. Donald L. Horowitz, *Ethnic Groups in Conflict* (Berkeley: University of California Press, 1985).

27. Chu, *Crafting Democracy*; Yun-han Chu, "The Realignment of State-Business Relations and Regime Transition in Taiwan," pp. 113-141 in Andrew MacIntyre, Ed., *Business and Government in Industrializing East and Southeast Asia* (Sydney: Allen & Unwin, 1994); Cheng-tian Kuo, *Global Competitiveness and Industrial Growth in Taiwan and the Philippines* (Pittsburgh: University of Pittsburgh Press, 1995); Cheng-tian Kuo, "Private Governance in Taiwan," pp. 84-95 in Steve Chan, Cal Clark, and Danny Lam, Eds., *Beyond the Developmental State: East Asia's Political Economies Reconsidered* (London: Macmillan, 1998).

28.   Chang-ling Huang, "Learning the New Game: Labor Politics in the Newly Democratized South Korea and Taiwan." Paper presented at the 2000 Annual Meeting of the American Political Science Association, Washington, D.C.

29.   Gold, *Taiwan Miracle*; Wachman, *National Identity*.

30.   Many in the United States, for example, fear that rising Taiwanese nationalism could destabilize the security situation in East Asia. See Ian Buruma, "Taiwan's New Nationalists," *Foreign Affairs* 75:4 (1996) pp. 77-91; Chas. W. Freeman, Jr., "Preventing War in the Taiwan Strait," *Foreign Affairs* 77:4 (1998) pp. 6-11.

31.   Gabriel A. Almond and G. Bingham Powell, Jr. Eds., *Comparative Politics Today: A World View* (Glenview, IL: Scott, Foresman, 1988); Peter Mair, *Party System Change: Approaches and Interpretations* (Oxford: Oxford University Press, 1997); G. Bingham Powell, Jr., *Contemporary Democracies: Participation, Stability, and Violence* (Cambridge: Harvard University Press, 1982); Giovanni Sartori, *Parties and Party Systems: A Framework for Analysis* (Cambridge: Cambridge University Press, 1976).

32.   Tun-jen Cheng and Yung-ming Hsu, "Issue Structure, the DPP's Factionalism, and Party Realignment," pp. 137-173 in Hung-mao Tien, Ed., *Taiwan's Electoral Politics and Democratic Transition: Riding the Third Wave* (Armonk, NY: M.E. Sharpe, 1996).

33.   Chao and Myers, *First Chinese Democracy*; Chu, *Crafting Democracy*; Hood, *Kuomintang*; Moody, *Political Change*.

34.   Cheng, "Taiwan in 1996;" Clark, "Presidential Election;" Tien, "Taiwan in 1995."

35.   Clark, "Presidential Elections;" John F. Copper, *Taiwan's 2000 Presidential and Vice Presidential Election: Consolidating Democracy and Creating a New Era of Politics* (Baltimore: School of Law, Maryland Series in Contemporary Asian Studies, 2000).

36.   Shelly Rigger, "Is Taiwan Independence *Passe*? Public Opinion, Party Platforms, and National Identity in Taiwan," in Chien-min Chao and Cal Clark, Eds., *The ROC on the Threshold of the 21ˢᵗ Century: A Paradigm Reexamined* (Baltimore: School of Law's Series in Contemporary Asian Studies, 1999) p. 48.

37.   Rigger, "Independence *Passe*?"

38.   Yun-han Chu and Tse-min Lin, "The Process of Democratic Consolidation in Taiwan: Social Cleavage, Electoral Competition, and the Emerging Party System," pp. 79-104 in Hung-mao Tien, Ed., *Taiwan's Electoral Politics and Democratic Transition: Riding the Third Wave* (Armonk, NY: M.E. Sharpe, 1996).

39.   Chao and Myers, The First Chinese Democracy; Chu, *Crafting Democracy*; Hood, *The Kuomintang*; Moody, *Political Change*; Wu, *Taiwan's Democratization*.

40.   Cheng, Taiwan in 1996; Higley, et al., "Elite Settlements;" Robinson, "Consensus Forged."

41.   Clark, "Presidential Elections;" Copper, *2000 Presidential and Vice Presidential Election*.

42.   Steve Chan, "Peace By Pieces? The Economic and Social Bases for 'Greater China.'" *American Asian Review* 14:2 (1996) pp. 35-50; Chu-yuan Cheng, "Economic Relations Across the Taiwan Straits: Mutual Dependence and Conflicts," pp. 63-83 in Winston L. Yang and Deborah A. Brown, Eds., *Across the Taiwan Strait: Exchanges, Conflicts, and Negotiations* (New York: Center for Asian

Studies, St. John's University, 1999); Peter C.Y. Chow "Complementarity and Competitiveness of the Economic Relations Across the Taiwan Strait: Problems and Prospects," pp. 173-189 in Winston L. Yang and Deborah A. Brown, Eds., *The Republic of China on Taiwan in the 1990s* (New York: Center for Asian Studies, St. John's University, 1997); Yu-shin Wu "Economic Reform, Cross-Straits Relations, and the Politics of Issue Linkage," pp. 111-133 in Ten-jen Cheng, Chi Huang, and Samuel S.G. Wu, Eds., *Inherited Rivalry: Conflict Across the Taiwan Straits* (Boulder, CO: Lynne Rienner, 1995).

43. Julian Baum, "Strait Talking," *Far Eastern Economic Review*, November 6, 1997, pp. 22-26; Clark, "Presidential Elections;" Leng, *Taiwan-China Connection*; Christopher R. Hughes, "Democratization and Beijing's Taiwan Policy," pp. 130-147 in Steve Tsang and Hung-mao Tien, Eds., *Democratization in Taiwan: Implications for China* (New York: St. Martin's, 1999).

44. Chao and Myers, *First Chinese Democracy*.

3 National Identity and Taiwan Security

CHIA-LUNG LIN

Taiwan has, in the last decade, undergone a full transition from authoritarianism to democracy. With Taiwan being an ethnically divided society under constant military threats, democracy building in Taiwan has been complicated by issues related to nation building and state building. In terms of identity politics, Taiwan's democracy building is characterized by the following triadic relations: the effort of the society's ethnic majority (native Taiwanese) to establish a new nation-state is resisted by an ethnic minority (Mainlander), whose desire to unify with its national homeland (Chinese Mainland) is echoed by the latter's readiness to end the identity dispute with force. Although the Taiwanese nationalism that arose during the democratic transition is liberal and pragmatic in nature, its rise has caused irrational reactions from the Chinese nationalists across the Taiwan Strait, thus posing a serious challenge to Taiwan's national security. This, if not well-handled, may endanger the stability and prospect of the new democracy.

This paper aims to analyze the impact of democratization on national identity and national security. The issues to be addressed here are the following: why the Taiwanese identity surges so quickly and what the implication is for Taiwan's national security. It will be argued that national identity is not inborn, but a socially and politically constructed sentiment that is subject to change, especially at times of regime transition. Electoral opening involved in the previously-excluded native Taiwanese into national politics and induced the opposition DPP (Democratic Progressive Party) to cultivate its social base through ethnic and nationalist mobilization. As a response, the incumbent KMT (Kuomintang) was driven to indigenize its ideology and power structure in order to dilute the influence of the opposition's ethnic and nationalist mobilization. Lee Teng-hui's redirection of the KMT's foreign and Mainland policies, as reflected in the "flexible diplomacy" and the "two-state theory," nonetheless raised tension across the Taiwan Strait, which in turn impacts Taiwan's national identity and national security. On the other hand, the Chinese Communist regime's increasing hostility toward Taiwan has given rise to a sense of common suffering among the people of Taiwan, who, regardless of their ethnic backgrounds, are forming a new national identity that is inclusive and civic in nature and a stronger desire to seek international recognition. On the other hand, Taiwan's quest for national identity and international recognition strongly irritates the Chinese Communists, who view these as steps toward separatism. With mutual trust absent and both sides unwilling to make a concession on the sovereignty issue, mostly due to constraints of domestic politics, the cross-strait tension may continue for quite some time.

The Surge of Taiwanese Nationalism

Taiwanese people's political identities have undergone significant changes in the past ten years, both in quality and quantity. In just one short decade, we witnessed how rapidly Taiwanese identity arose and Chinese identity dwindled, as well as how rapidly support for Taiwan independence climb at the expense of that for Chinese unification. According to the earliest national survey data one could find, as recent as 1989, only 16% of the interviewees considered themselves Taiwanese while 52% self-identified as Chinese and another 26% considered themselves both a Chinese and a Taiwanese (or both a Taiwanese and a Chinese).[1] However, as Taiwan's political democratization furthered, people's identity also began to change. Various popular surveys have indicated that those who self-identify as Taiwanese have outnumbered those with Chinese identity since 1994[2] and the gap continues to widen (see Figure 1).[3]

Another phenomenon worth noticing in Figure 3.1 is that there continues to be around 40% of the population who consider themselves both a Chinese and a Taiwanese. A logical explanation might be that some of those who previously self-identified as Chinese are now willing to admit that they are Taiwanese also, but their strong attachment to China makes it difficult for them to abandon their Chinese identity. Having dual identities seems to be a more comfortable choice for these people, at least for the time being.

Besides making a national identity change, many people have also changed their preference on the ultimate arrangement of the cross-strait political relations (i.e., unification vs. independence). As recent as 1989, a survey conducted by the *United Daily* on the people's stateness preference

Figure 3.1 Changes of Taiwanese People's National Identity

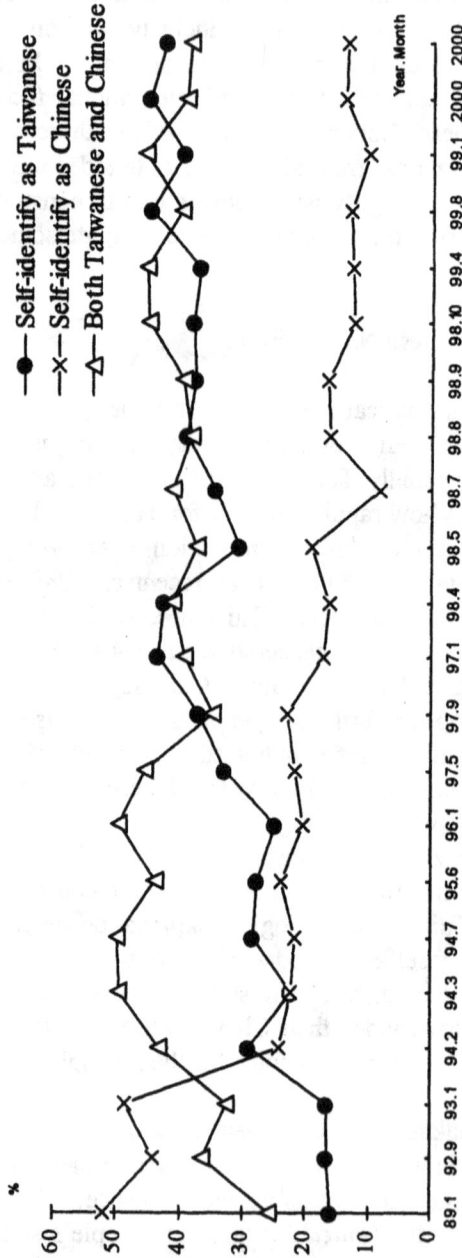

found that 55% of the interviewees thought that Taiwan should become an independent country.[4] These figures have nonetheless changed quite significantly following Taiwan's recent political development. A similar survey conducted by the *United Daily* in 1994 already found higher support for independence than for unification. Data of the past two to three years show that independence supporters and unification supporters constitute around 30% and 20% of the population, respectively, while another 30-40% prefer the status quo.[5]

After ten years of democratization, Taiwanese people's support for unification has dropped significantly. But, what is worth noticing is that the independence movement, though gradually gaining popularity, is still far from securing majority support because about one-third of the population still prefers the status quo. Even though advocating the status quo is in essence the same as supporting the view that Taiwan and the Mainland should continue to remain separated and governed by two different governments, these status quo advocates apparently are more concerned than the independent supporters about the danger of declaring Taiwan independence. This is particularly true for Mainlanders in Taiwan. It is interesting to note that, while the sharp decline in support for unification has been a common phenomenon within the native Taiwanese and within Mainlanders, only very few Mainlanders turn to endorse Taiwan independence, with most of whom finding it more comfortable to support the status quo and remain a realist.

The awakening of autonomous consciousness among the native Taiwanese and the deepening sense of crises among Mainlanders have made identity politics the most salient issue on Taiwan's national agenda since the onset of democratization. The issue of nationalism is sensitive and disturbing not only in that it touches a chord in people's historical memory but because it is closely linked to Taiwan's national security and political future. To find out whether the nationalism issue will endanger Taiwan's democratic development, we need to first probe the nature of Taiwanese and Chinese identities and examine whether they are competitive or complementary in nature. More specifically, we need to understand whether the nationalizing Taiwanese state is ethnicity-based and may repress the minority Mainlanders, whether the Mainlanders, whose privileges gradually faded during Taiwan's democratization, may turn to seek support from across the Taiwan Strait, and whether people of different identities can agree to determine Taiwan's political future democratically, respect the basic rights of one another, and tolerate opposing nationalist voices.

Fortunately, recent development has been somewhat encouraging. While the people of Taiwan still lack a strong consensus on what the ultimate Taiwan-Mainland relations should be, empirical data have suggested that the rising Taiwanese identity is not an ethnicity-based primordial identity, but a civic political identity which many people find comfortable to embrace.[6]

Although there is a high correlation between one's ethnic identity and national identity, one should not equate the two. For instance, not all Mainlanders lack Taiwanese consciousness and not all native Taiwanese embrace Taiwanese identity. In addition, it is important to point out that the terms "Taiwanese" and "Chinese" may mean differently to different people and their meanings may also change along with their context change. Interviews conducted by the author found that people in Taiwan tend to define "Taiwanese" using territorial/political or subjective/psychological criteria and define "Chinese" using primordial/cultural criteria.[7]

This finding has important implication for Taiwan's political development. One way to reconcile the differences between Taiwanese and Chinese identity and minimize their conflicts is for one to treat his/her Chinese identity as a cultural expression (i.e., *hua jen*) or an ethnic origin (i.e., *han jen*) and to treat his/her Taiwanese identity as a political identity that is shared by a group of people living in the same political territory with same citizenship. As long as those with Chinese identity do not deny Taiwan as a sovereign political entity, whether an independent state or a geographical territory, whether under the name "Republic of China" or "Republic of Taiwan," and as long as those with Taiwanese identity do not deny the fact that the Chinese culture and the Han people have constituted a large portion of the Taiwanese culture and the Taiwanese people, then the surge of Taiwanese identity would not necessarily intensify ethnic conflicts on the island and bring about political confrontations across the Taiwan Strait.

Nationalism and Liberal Democracy

To what extent the rise of Taiwanese identity be an obstruction to Taiwan's democratic development will largely depend on two factors: first, whether the people can form a basic consensus on the boundary of their state; second, whether the people are willing to solve Taiwan's "stateness" disputes via democratic procedures.[8] After all, a liberal democracy is founded on the principle of majority rule and protecting minority rights. The ultimate test to see if a liberal democracy can consolidate in a divided society like Taiwan lies in whether people of different national identities can learn to trust one another and tolerate collective allegiances drastically from their own.

Questions 1 and 2 in Table 3.1 show how people with different national identities define the territory and citizenship of their country (whether it is called Republic of China or Taiwan). In early 1996, the Taiwanese people still had no strong consensus on whether the territory of their country covers only Taiwan (and its neighboring islands) or extends to cover the Chinese Mainland as well. There was also no strong consensus on whether "citizens of their country" refer only to the 21 million people of Taiwan or include the 1.2 billion people on the Mainland. By mid 1996, however, 51% of the people already came to a more realistic view that their territory does not cover the Chinese mainland, thus acknowledging the de facto independence of the "ROC on Taiwan." But 33% of the people still thought that their state territory covered the Chinese mainland. As to citizenship, 58% of the people believed that it should only include the 21 million people of Taiwan and 28% argued that the 1.2 billion people on the Mainland were also citizens of their country.

Question 3 asked the interviewees who they thought would have the right to determine Taiwan's future; the people showed a stronger consensus on this question. In mid-1996, 73% of the interviewees thought that only the 21 million people of Taiwan have the right to determine Taiwan's future, a view even shared by most people who self-identify as Chinese (64%) and as Chinese and Taiwanese (70%) (see Table 3.2). In other words, contrary to their definition of the country's territory and citizenship, most people with Chinese identity indeed viewed the island as the legitimate boundary for making fundamental political decisions such as determining the future of Taiwan. According to a mid-1998 survey, supports for the realistic views on the three questions related to territory, citizenship, and sovereignty further climbed to 65%, 64%, and 81%, respectively, a 20% jump in just two and half years.

Question 4 explored whether the people considered it appropriate that Taiwan's future be determined via plebiscite. It turns out that most interviewees actually supported the idea of using plebiscite to solve "stateness" disputes. Over the years, support for plebiscite climbed from 52% in 1993 to 68% in 1996, and then dropped slightly to 60% in 1998.

Table 3.1 How Taiwan's People Perceive Their Territory, Citizenship, Sovereignty and Legitimacy of Plebiscite

	Feb. 1993	Feb. 1996	July 1996	July 1998
1. **Territory** Do you think the territory of our state should only include Taiwan and its neighboring islands or should it include the Mainland also?	---	41% / 42%	51% / 33%	65% / 27%
2. **Citizenship** Do you think the citizens of our state should only include the 21 million people on Taiwan and its neighboring islands or should the 12 billion people on the Mainland also be included?	---	44% / 39%	58% / 28%	64% / 28%
3. **Sovereignty** Do you think only the people of Taiwan have the right to decide Taiwan's future or do you think the people on the Mainland also have the right to participate?	---	---	73% / 13%	81% / 13%
4. **Plebiscite** Do you agree or disagree to solve Taiwan's stateness issue via plebiscite?	52% / 28%	56% / 23%	68% / 17%	60% / 34%
5. **Plebiscite** Will you accept or not accept a plebiscite result that differs from your stateness preference?	---	---	---	70%/20%

Note: In "A% : B%," A% denotes those who think their territory, citizenship and sovereignty only cover Taiwan and its neighboring islands and B% denotes those who think the Mainland should also be included.

Source: The 1993 and two 1996 surveys were conducted by Workshop 306 at the Political Science Department of National Taiwan University and the effective sample sizes were 1398, 1376, and 1406, respectively. The 1998 telephone survey was conducted by Chuan Hsiun Company, with an effective sample size of 1027.

An encouraging discovery is that the majority of Chinese nationalists do not reject the idea of using plebiscite to solve critical national issues despite their fear of a majority plebiscite result favoring Taiwan independence. Interestingly, when asked whether they will accept a plebiscite result that differs from their own stance on the statehood issue, only 20% of the interviewees showed reservation while 70% openly expressed their willingness to accept a majority decision (see Question 5).

Table 3.2 How Taiwan's People Perceive Their Country's Territory, Citizenship and Sovereignty, by National Identity (July 1996)

	I am Taiwanese n=557	I am Taiwanese and Chinese n=605	I am Chinese n=208
1. Territory (1) Our territory only covers Taiwan and its neighboring islands.	66%	46%	32%
(2) Our territory also includes the Mainland	15%	42%	56%
2. Citizenship (1) Our citizens only cover the 21 million people on Taiwan and its neighboring islands.	72%	52%	41%
(2) Our citizens also include the 12 billion people on the Mainland China.	11%	36%	47%
3. Sovereignty (1) Only the people of Taiwan have the right to determine Taiwan's future.	81%	70%	64%
(2) The people on the Chinese Mainland also have the right to determine Taiwan's future	5%	17%	25%

Source: Same as Table 3.1.

Given Taiwan's domestic and international situation, a gradualist approach to the "stateness" issue seems most acceptable to most people on Taiwan. And political reality also seems to prevent both Taiwanese and Chinese nationalists from pursuing their nationalist goals with a strong sense of urgency because Taiwan has long enjoyed a *de facto* independence and was never for one day ruled by the People's Republic of China. To them, what to strive for is not a separation from the PRC, but a *de jure* recognition from the international community. Therefore, as long as Taiwan retains its sovereignty and keeps marching toward a full democracy, most Taiwanese nationalists will find no urgency to declare independence in the immediate future. On the other hand, to most Chinese nationalists, a speedy unification is unrealistic due to the huge social, economic and political disparities across the strait. Chinese nationalists in Taiwan identify with the Chinese nation, not the Chinese Communist regime. Since the mainland is still ruled by the Communist Party, pursuing a prompt unification with the mainland will man surrendering a new democracy to a communist regime.

Since neither Taiwanese nationalists nor Chinese nationalists consider it urgent to pursue their nationalist goal at all costs and to push for a final settlement in the immediate future, the status quo is likely to be prolonged for quite some time. As long as the "stateness" issue remains unsettled, Taiwan's political future will continue to be filled with uncertainties.

Dynamics of Nation Formation

Why did the Taiwanese nationalism surge during Taiwan's transition to democracy and why has it acquired a high degree of civic and liberal nature? First, one can argue that the seed of Taiwanese nationalism was already deeply planted during the Japanese colonial rule and the post-War political reconstruction. Second, one should pay attention to the epic changes in the international system since the late 1970s that the first precipitated the state legitimacy crisis and later aroused the aspiration for an independent statehood. However, I argue that neither historical and global forces on people's political consciousness must be actualized through state actions, competing elite's strategies, and their mutual influences and compromises. I argue that national identities are not inborn but are socially and politically constructed sentiments that are subject to political mobilization and manipulation. While it is natural that people develop a sense of group consciousness after a long period of territorial isolation and social integration, any sudden change of group identity certainly calls for a political explanation.[9]

Throughout the post-War era, the state-directed formation of Chinese nationality continued to run into arduous resistance from certain quarters of the native society, especially from victim families of the February 28th Incident, overseas Taiwanese in exile, and members of the Presbyterian church. The resistance had its historical roots. The development of a distinctive Taiwanese identity and its ensuing quest for an independent statehood were fostered by two related historical antecedents. The first is the 50 years of Japanese colonial rule, during which the native elite were first subjected to a state-orchestrated de-sinicization campaign and later a naturalization program that was proceeded in full gear during the last few years of World War II. Japan's colonial rule facilitated Taiwan's early acquisition of a semi-peripheral position relative to China through state-directed modernization programs. And the interests of the native Taiwanese elite were incorporated into Japan's military and economic conquest of peripheral countries, including China, in the so-called Great East Asian Co-Prosperity Zone.[10] The second is the "birth defect" incurred during Taiwan's de-colonization and the KMT's establishment of Chinese rule after the war. This birth defect, epitomized by the February 28th Incidence, along with the imposed political subordination, precipitated the formation of Taiwan independence movement among Taiwanese in exile. Despite many shared ethnic heritages between the native Taiwanese and the newly arrived Mainlanders, the birth defect also attenuated the state's effort to establish the supremacy of Chinese identity over local identity through re-sinicization and Mandarinization programs.[11] As soon as the political domination was loosened, the long-suppressed Taiwanese identity quickly re-emerged.

Taiwanese nationalism has surged also in part because the KMT's claim of its representation of the Chinese Mainland crumbled in the late 1970s in a series of de-recognition crises and because the formation of the new world order beginning in the late 1980s provided a window of opportunity for the admission of new states. For an extended period following the outbreak of the Korean War, the ROC's precarious sovereign status was sustained essentially by the U.S. hegemony and its post-war security arrangements. It was the U.S.-harbored international recognition and American security commitment that elongated the ROC's diminishing international status until the end of 1979. The PRC-U.S. rapprochement in early 1970s set off a series of diplomatic setbacks for Taiwan -- the loss of the U.N. seat to the PRC, the expulsion from all major international organizations, and de-recognition by major allies. These external shocks severely undermined the KMT's long-standing claim that the ROC government is the sole legitimate government of the whole China and weakened its entrenched one-party authoritarian regime. Next came the breakup of the Eastern bloc, which was accompanied by a resurgence of ethnic and national strife. In the transition to the post-Cold War era, the political and territorial integrity of many existing states was seriously challenged. In many instances, the international community was seemingly perceptive to the claims of certain collective entities of their rights to self-determination, autonomy, or secession. At the same time, the emerging structural configuration of the Asia-Pacific security order also gives Taiwan some room for diplomatic maneuvering because the long-term goals of China, a major power aspirant, may be potentially in conflict with those of the U.S. and Japan. These developments have raised new hope for an independent Taiwanese statehood.

However, both the growth potential of the historical seeds and the transformative potential of the soc-called "new world order" would not have brought about a fundamental shift in people's group identity had there not been succession crisis within the KMT, electoral opening at the national level, and intensified tension across the Taiwan Strait. In Taiwan, democratization has served as a *pulling* force, drawing people together through the process of political participation, which not only creates in them a sense of loyalty to the political system, but generates multiple issues that are of interest to different groups, thus offering them an incentive to form various cross-cutting coalitions on different issues, with no groups or interests able to permanently dominate other groups or interests. If the existence of a nation is, in the words of Ernest Renan, "an everyday plebiscite,[12] then the practice of democracy in Taiwan definitely serves to nurture their sense of belonging to a civic nation."

On the other hand, the PRC's hostility toward democratizing Taiwan has served as a *pushing* force. The PRC's long-existing and ever-growing threat has fostered a sense of common destiny that is shared by a great majority of people in Taiwan regardless of ethnic backgrounds. Again, drawing on Renan, having suffered together actually weighs more in the formation of a nation than the sharing of triumph because suffering imposes obligation and demands common efforts, which later become a collective memory that is part of each individual's life. Together, the pulling and pushing forces have interacted to lead the people of Taiwan, who are in search of a collective identity, to gradually develop a more inclusive civic identity (which Juan Linz calls "state-nation"[13] that looks forward to what the new democracy must be, rather than backward to the unrealized ideal of building either a unified Chinese nation-state or an independent Taiwanese nation-state.

The impact of Taiwan's democratization on its nation formation can be examined at both mass and elite levels. At the mass level, political democratization, especially the opening of national elections, serves as a whirlpool involving all people of Taiwan into the same political process and driving social groups with different interests and identities to communicate, negotiate and compromise. With democratization came the opening of political society. Through voting and elections, participating in party affairs and social movements, coming into contact with politicians, reading and listening to the press, and discussing among relatives, friends and colleagues, people begin to feel a sense of belonging to a common political community.

If the birth of a nation must use certain rituals to symbolize and forge group consciousness, then in Taiwan's case, no collective ritual is more impressive than the holding of elections, both in terms of frequency, extensiveness, and intensity. When the Taiwanese people periodically participate in the elections of their President and Legislature, they are in essence consenting the existence of a state that they all belong to and accepting this island as the legitimate boundary for calculating votes. In other words, political democratization presumes the existence of a state and, through participating in national affairs, the people are jointly creating a state-nation. If a nation is, according to Benedict Anderson (1991), an "imagined" community, then the community imagined by the people of Taiwan is most likely to be comprised of those on the island, not on the Mainland, because the boundaries of their daily social, economic and political activities all coincide with the physical boundary of an island called Taiwan.

The impact of cross-strait relations on Taiwan's nation formation has to do with war. Along with democratization also came increasing cross-strait contacts as well as the people's realization of the huge gap in political values and institutions across the strait. Because the Chinese Communist regime has refused to give up the possibility of taking over Taiwan with force, direct cross-strait contacts actually help the people further apprehend how real the animosity is. Facing China's military threats, the Taiwanese people have gradually developed a sense of common suffering. To defend their hard-earned well-being and democracy, the people are forced to set aside their internal differences and to place national security above party and ethnic interests. As public opinion surveys reveal, there continues to be a positive correlation between the rise in cross-strait tensions and the people's identification with Taiwan.[14]

Identity is a matter of similarities vs. differences, a matter of relative distance. Empirical data have shown that, in the minds of most Taiwanese people, differences between the two sides of the Taiwan Strait are far greater than those among groups with different national identities in Taiwan.[15] Whether the perception reflects the reality, this psychological distance indeed has a profound impact on the formation of Taiwanese nationalism. As Walker Connor (1994: 75) highlights, "it is not what is, but what *people believe* is that has behavioral consequences." For one thing, when put on the same scale, the psychological chasm across the strait inevitably makes the identity problems within Taiwan look relatively trivial. And, because the Mainland culture is perceived to be more authoritarian and uncivil, people of all ethnic backgrounds in Taiwan, especially those with unpleasant encounters with the Mainland Chinese, are induced to embrace the more liberal and democratic culture that is taking shape on the island.[16]

Lee Teng-hui and Cross-Strait Relations

To well explain the surge of Taiwanese nationalism since the early 1990s, we have to turn our attention to the role of the political elites in the construction of new group identity, for political elites are by nature specialists in the mobilization of grievance and hope, especially on the issue of nationalism. From early on, DPP leaders have built their electoral support upon the native Taiwanese people's shared sense of deprivation and misery. The DPP leadership played up the issue because this salient cleavage cuts across socioeconomic strata. Nationalism was viewed as an effective counter strategy to the KMT's broadly-based socio-economic development program and an issue that could unite the DPP supporters of different social and economic interests under a common cause.[17] However it was the power struggle within the KMT after the passing of Chiang Ching-kuo that critically turned the tide against the prevailing official ideological claim on Chinese identity. The intra-party struggle came to a point of no return in early 1990, when Lee Teng-hui was challenged by his Mainlander rivals in the KMT's party nomination for presidential candidate. It was also the turning point for the growth of Taiwanese nationalism.

Although Lee Teng-hui was extremely cautious in playing the role of a nominal leader during the first two years of his presidency, various Mainlander factions still held him personally responsible for their loss of power and the rise of Taiwanese independence movement. The 1990 presidential election provided the anti-Lee forces a timely opportunity to jointly challenge Lee's leadership. However, the social unrest stirred by the power struggle within the KMT eventually led to a massive student movement, demanding for a thorough political reform. Faced with challenges from inside and outside the party, Lee made a critical decision to collaborate with the pro-reform forces in pushing for democratization. By inviting the opposition to participate in the cross-party National Affairs Conference, Lee not only successfully isolated the conservative camp, but also legitimatized his reform plans, including abrogating the Temporary Provision, revising the Constitution, and re-electing national representatives.

At this moment, Lee knew quite well that once democratization began its course, the confrontation between Taiwanese nationalism and Chinese nationalism would quickly surface because there was no more reason to exclude anyone from participating in the democratic process. To ease resistance of Chinese nationalists on the island and to maintain stability across the Taiwan Strait, Lee made another crucial decision soon after the holding of the National Affairs Conference, that is, the establishment of the National Unification Council under the Presidential Office. The Council later issued a set of National Unification Guidelines, which views Taiwan (ROC) and mainland China (PRC) as two parallel political entities (states) and divides the pursuit of a unified China into three stages (short term, mid term and long term). The strategic thinking behind Lee's announcing of the Guidelines was to provide a functional framework for maintaining domestic and international stability so as to buy time for Taiwan's democratization and his power consolidation.[18]

Basically, Lee Teng-hui adopted a pragmatic approach toward the issue of nationalism. Though considering Taiwan as an independent state and cross-strait relations as "state-to-state" relations, Lee was very careful in dealing with unification vs. independence disputes, trying to keep the symbol of ROC intact in order to prevent strong reactions from Chinese nationalists. By re-interpreting and revising the ROC Constitution, Lee was able to smoothly conduct Taiwan's transition to democracy and adjust its national status. Between 1991 and 1996, Taiwan held three constitutional revisions, two National Assembly elections, two Legislative elections, and one direct presidential election. These elections realized the ideal of rule by the people. At the same time, the people began to form a Taiwan-centered national identity and the government eventually admitted that the sovereignty of the ROC only covers Taiwan and its neighboring islands.

The advancement of democratization made the KMT more sensitive to the society's yearning for self-identity, international recognition, and a secure future. However, had it not been under Lee Teng-hui's political leadership, the KMT would have had a much harder time transforming itself and surviving electoral competitions. On his way to power consolidation, Lee skillfully shifted the burden of defending the orthodox lines to his Mainlander rivals, such as upholding the extra-constitutional arrangements amid a global wave of democratization, advocating the obsolete One China principle when the world has de-recognized the ROC as a legitimate state, and protecting the Chinese identity against the rising Taiwanese consciousness. On the other hand, being a native Taiwanese, Lee's installation of the regime's democratization and indigenization had allowed him to dislodge the KMT's ideological constraints and launch a series of bold foreign policy initiatives. By adopting the so-called "pragmatic diplomacy" or "flexible democracy," Lee not only successfully absorbed the DPP's main agenda (such as bidding for U.N. membership and normalizing cross-strait relations), thus diluting its mobilization capacity in this regard, but revitalized the immigrant KMT regime, thus helping to preserve its electoral dominance.

Lee Teng-hui's redirection of the KMT's foreign and Mainland policies, while contributing to the regime's electoral survival, had a spillover effect on the cross-strait relations, which had tensed up in part due to the government's enthusiastic pursuit of independent sovereignty and international recognition. The evolution of cross-strait relations can be better understood using a two-level-game approach, a framework Robert Putnam (1998) suggested for analyzing the interactions of domestic and international politics, who observes that "clever players will spot a move on one board that will trigger realignment on the other boards."[19] In Putnam's metaphor, statesmen are strategically position between two "tables," one representing domestic politics and the other international negotiation. Diplomatic tactics and strategies are constrained simultaneously by what other states will accept and what domestic constituencies will ratify. A negotiation is successful only if the statesmen can both reach an international agreement and secure its domestic ratification.

Looking retrospectively, Lee Teng-hui's adoption of a somewhat ambiguous "ROC on Taiwan" approach was crucial in making Taiwan's democratization and internationalization compatible and complementary to each other's advancement. Lee's decision to link Taiwan's internationalization to its democratization was certainly a calculated political action. He realized that although the One China principle had become a burden to Taiwan's democratization, it was also a necessary cover for continuing Taiwan's democratization and for adjusting cross-strait relations. As Lee Teng-hui gradually completed Taiwan's transition to democracy and broadened his power base, he became bold enough to push for Taiwan's international participation and redefine the cross-strait relations as a "state-to-state relationship." with the ROC and PRC having non-overlapping jurisdictions over Taiwan and the Mainland, respectively.

Beginning in 1993, when cross-strait relations were in a relatively peaceful mode due to the holding of a quasi-official cross-strait talk after decades of separation and hostility, Lee made a critical move to openly endorse the issue of "joining the U.N." and place it high on the national agenda. Domestically, the bid for U.N. membership not only increased Lee's popularity, but also served to marginalize KMT conservatives (and the New Party) and paved by the way for the forming a tacit KMT-DPP coalition. Internationally, although the chance of Taiwan obtaining an U.N. membership was extremely slim in the short term, this issue had put Beijing on the defensive side when it tried to block Taiwan's participation in the international arena.

Lee's pursuit of pragmatic diplomacy stemmed from two major concerns: one was to raise Taiwan's bargaining power in its negotiations with the PRC and the other was to maximize the KMT's chance of electoral survival. By involving the people into the process of policy making through democratization and by increasing Taiwan's visibility through internationalization, what Lee was trying to accomplish was to influence the timing, agenda-setting and outcome of the final settlement with the PRC on the sovereignty issue. Equally important, the pragmatic approach toward Taiwan's national status and international participation also served the

KMT's political interests quite well. Lee was probably quite aware that, although the Taiwanese people were eager in seeking international recognition, in the face of the PRC's military threat, the KMT's moderate "ROC on Taiwan" approach would be less risky and more acceptable to most Taiwanese people than the radical approaches of the DPP and NP.

Whether intended or not, Lee's pragmatic diplomacy, especially his 1995 visit to the U.S., drove Beijing to further tighten its grips on Taiwan's outreaching efforts. Concerned that the improvement of the U.S.-Taiwan relations might set in motion chain reactions in the international community, the Chinese leadership decided to teach Taiwan a lesson and demonstrate to the U.S. its non-negotiable position on the One China principle. In the months following Lee's visit to the U.S., Beijing withdrew its ambassador to the U.S., terminated a few ongoing U.S.-China projects, forced a number of countries to de-recognize the ROC government, pressured several international organizations to turn down Taiwan's membership applications, and even launched a series of military exercises and missile test surrounding Taiwan. Beijing's signal was clear: the more Taiwan tries to reach out, the higher the cost it has to pay.

China's military intimidation nonetheless turned out to be counterproductive. It not only greatly irritated the Taiwanese people but forced the US to send two aircraft carriers to protect Taiwan during the 1996 presidential election. In fact, China's increasing hostility only drove the Taiwanese people, either out of concern for national security or national dignity, to rally behind President Lee. As empirical data revealed, come voters eventually shifted to vote for Lee out of strategic calculations.[20] As Hsu Hsin-liang, then DPP chairman, commented after the election, the increasing cross-strait tension turned Taiwan into a "society in constant crisis," a situation, he argued, was conducive to the incumbent's remaining in power.

The PRC's military aggressiveness toward Taiwan, especially during the 1996 presidential election, also poses a threat to the regional security of the Asia-Pacific. Beijing's readiness to use force in solving international disputes alarmed the international community, especially the U.S. and Japan. Although the U.S. still maintains that it will not intrude in cross-strait relations, its sending of battleships has nonetheless made its policy of "strategic ambiguity" hard to sustain.[21] Immediately after the crisis was over, the U.S. and Japan decided to speed up the revision of the U.S.- Japan Mutual Security Treaty, which vaguely defines "crisis in the neighborhood" (being ambiguous was an attempt not to irritate China) so as to leave room for possible inclusion of future cross-strait conflicts into the applicable domain of the treaty. Looking from a two-level-game perspective, Lee's skillful linkage of foreign policy (internationalization) and domestic policy (democratization) had not only helped him consolidate his power domestically, but triggered a dramatic change in the regional security environment.

The 1996 cross-strait crisis was a turning point in the U.S.-China-Taiwan relations. On the one hand, Taiwan's democratic transition was now complete and its people could no longer tolerate vaguely defined national characteristics and being deprived of international participation. On the other hand, the Chinese Communists, being in the stage of leadership succession struggle and faced with the returns of Hong Kong and Macao, found it especially difficult to tolerate Taiwan's search for national independence. The U.S. therefore became the key-determining factor in the cross-strait tug-of -war. However, the U.S. did not seem so psychologically well prepared to face this challenge. From Taiwan's point of view, if the U.S. recognizes Taiwan's democratic efforts, it should also accept the reality that the ROC on Taiwan is in fact an independent state, adjust accordingly its One China policy (constructed based on the three communiqués issued during the cold war period), and give Taiwan an appropriate degree of international recognition. However, when Lee Teng-hui was working hard with Taiwan's democracy-building projects, the Clinton Administration was only focused on engaging China. After all, to maintain its hegemony, the U.S. needs to have China's cooperation on issues such as arms control, non-proliferation, the Korean issue, Middle and South Asia conflicts, and sovereignty disputes in the South China Sea, etc., not to mention the economic gains the U.S. can get from the Chinese market. As a result, a paradox surfaced. That is, as Taiwan's popular opinion was moving further away from China, the U.S. government was making closer ties with the Chinese authority. At the end, Lee Teng-hui was forced to issue the two-state theory to defend Taiwan's position.

After the 1996 crisis, China learned that the cross-strait issue cannot be resolved without taking the international environment into account. In April of 1996, China began to establish a strategic partnership with Russia by launching the so-called, "superpower diplomacy." Later, it further extended its partnership relations to India, France, England, and Japan. And when Jiang Zemin visited the U.S. in October 1997, the two governments signed a "constructive strategic partnership" communiqué. Another function that China's superpower diplomacy served was to "transcend the Taiwan problem so as to solve it." By establishing partnerships with major nations, China hopes to blockade Taiwan's pragmatic diplomacy through three approaches, namely, break all of Taiwan's formal diplomatic ties, block all of Taiwan's entrances to international politics, and strip all of Taiwan's loses all of its diplomatic recognition and international support, it will only be unable to join the United Nations, but also be forced by international superpowers to enter a unification talk with China.

China realizes that the closest way to prevent Taiwan from moving toward independence is through Washington. After the 1996 crisis, China made every effort to ask the U.S. to accept the so-called "three no's policy," namely, no support for Taiwan independence, no support for "one China, one Taiwan" or "two Chinas," and no support for Taiwan's joining international organizations where statehood is a prerequisite. The opportunity came in July of 1998 when Clinton made a state visit to China. On his way to Shanghai, Clinton mentioned in a non-official meeting that the US has a "three-no's policy" toward Taiwan. The biggest damage the three no's policy does to Taiwan is that it deprives the Taiwanese participation in international organizations where statehood is a requirement has allowed China to treat Taiwan as Hong Kong (China's domestic political entity). Having successfully forced the U.S. into announcing its three no's policy, China further turned to demand the same policy from other superpowers. And Russia even agreed to a fourth no, that is, no arms sales to Taiwan. By weakening Taiwan's self-defense capacity, China is paving the way for unifying Taiwan with the use of force.

In October 1998, delegates from Taiwan and China had their second, long-halted Koo-Wang talk in Beijing. While Beijing hoped to define the meeting as a political negotiation, so as to impress the world that the two sides of the Taiwan Strait was beginning to conduct unification talks, in Taiwan there is a lack of a domestic consensus on what the meeting should focus on. On the day before Taiwan's delegation departed for Beijing, Lee Teng-hui instructed the delegates that "democracy" and "parity" should be two top principles in the forthcoming cross-strait meeting. He also wanted the delegates to remind Beijing that Taiwan was returned to the Republic of China in 1945 per the Postdam Proclamation and that since the PRC was founded in 1949, the jurisdictions of the two governments have never overlapped, so "a separately governed China" is an undeniable fact. In Lee

Teng-hui's thinking, the importance of the Koo-Wang talk is not to reach any concrete agreement, but to use China's stage to let the world hear Taiwan's voice.[22]

After the second Koo-Wang talk, Lee Teng-hui decided to set up a "Strengthen the ROC Sovereignty Research Team" to study how to remind the international society of the fact that Taiwan is a sovereign independent state, and how to consolidate the legal basis of this fact with international and domestic laws, and how to ensure an equal negotiation status in the upcoming third Koo-Wang Talk.[23] In Lee's thinking, since cross-strait political negotiations seemed to be unavoidable, Taiwan might as well use the negotiations to highlight the fact that the two sides of the strait are of equal, state-to-state relations, so as to secure a better bargaining position for Taiwan. The strategic significance fo Lee's two-state theory lies in that instead of following the traditional One China framework imposed by the PRC and endorsed by the U.S., which considers any new move a change in the status quo, the theory tries to clarify what the status quo really is.

Defending Taiwan's Democracy

The recent escalation of cross-strait tension has raised the concerns of many on Taiwan's national security, worrying whether the new democracy can defend itself when China does launch military attacks. Indeed, history has seen many instances where democracies broke down under military interventions, severe economic shocks, and social disorders. From a comparative perspective, Taiwan has been a strange democracy, not endowed with the fortune of being able to control its own political destiny. But, it does have all the conditions of being an independent country except for international recognition. Taiwan's quest for a *de jure* independence will definitely not come easy because the PRC has deemed Taiwan an inseparable part of China and threatened to resort to military solutions if independence is declared. And China's readiness to impose its will through flexing military muscles has made the cross-strait issue more than a matter of moral justice, but a source of uncertainty that may impact the Asia-Pacific security.

As long as threats from China exist, Taiwan's national security will remain a test to its democratic stability. First of all, as Taiwan gradually marches toward a full democracy, it also slowly inches toward *de jure* independence, a move that will certainly call for a higher degree of national defense and international support. However, Taiwan finds itself in a security dilemma because if it tries to strengthen its national security (e.g., via improving foreign relations and upgrading weaponry), China will very likely react with an even harsher measure, and the Taiwanese people will feel less secure and will wish further strengthen its national security.

Second, Taiwan's increasing economic dependence on China will make Taiwan's domestic politics somewhat vulnerable to China's intervention and manipulation (some achieved via its lobby groups in Taiwan). Here is yet another dilemma. If Taiwan insists on maintaining its political autonomy, it might find the economic consequences unbearable, but if it tries to take advantages of China's enormous market, then the economic dependence might subject its national security to certain risks.

Third, while national security is a necessary condition for consolidating a new democracy that is constantly under foreign threats, a heavy concentration of national resources on national defense can nonetheless take away the resources needed for economic and social reforms, thus limiting the chance of the new democracy to demonstrate its efficacy. Though this might not be too serious a dilemma, Taiwan still needs to find an appropriate balance for resource allocation, so that national security could be defended no at the cost of democratic progress.

Can a democratic Taiwan better defend itself under the threat of the non-democratic China? The impact of democratization on Taiwan's national security seems to be a double edged sword.   On the positive side, democratization has involved the people into the process of policy formation, nurtured a sense of civic identity among them, and fostered a national consensus on Taiwan's necessity to participate in the international community.   Moreover, the fact that the people's consensus is built on democracy, freedom and self-determination also gives Taiwan's quest for international participation a morally justifiable cause that is hard to be ignored by other liberal democracies.

On the other hand, one possible drawback of practicing democracy and open-economy in a society under constant foreign threat is that its national security may be subject to hostile foreign manipulation. This is true particularly after Taiwan and China enter the World Trade Organization and the "three links" becoming a reality. The deepening economic dependence on China has introduced into Taiwan diverse and sometimes conflicting interests, which not only reduce its state autonomy but also make the decision-making process less efficient and foreign policy outputs less coherent.

While Taiwan's political destiny is controlled as much by others as by itself, there are actually a few things Taiwan can work on to preserve its democracy and even keep it flourishing. First of all, the government needs to further strengthen its legitimacy and performance so as to nurture the people's trust and confidence in the new democracy. By doing so, the people of Taiwan will eventually internalize democratic values and apply these values in solving critical national affairs, even as crucial as the issue of independence vs. unification. Second, the people also need to forge a greater consensus on national identity and national security, to know what they want and how to go about it when the cross-strait situations call for a final settlement. Most importantly, with Asia-Pacific going through a rapid power realignment, Taiwan needs to redefine its role in relation to the region's major powers (the U.S., China, Japan, and the ASEAN) and find a niche for its survival and development, both geo-politically and economically. Third, through more actively participating in international organizations and events, whether officially or unofficially, Taiwan can make its democratic future an international concern. It is especially crucial that Taiwan strengthens its relations with the U.S. (including the government, mass media and general public) because it is the only hegemon that has the capacity to unilaterally guarantee peace and stability in the Asia-Pacific.

Notes

1. Data were adopted from telephone interviews conducted by the Survey Center of the *United Daily* (see *United Daily*, Nov. 29,1989).
2. As the author detailed in other works, Taiwanese consciousness and support for independence have picked up their momentum since 1994, probably due to increasing cross-strait interactions and tensions (Chia-lung Lin: 1998,1999).
3. Besides the survey commissioned by the Mainland Affairs Council of Executive Yuan, surveys conducted by the *United Daily*, *China Times*, and the Democratic Progressive Party also had similar findings.
4. *United Daily* (Nov. 29, 1989).
5. Chia-lung Lin (1998:508, 542).
6. For details, see Chia-lung Lin (1999).
7. Chia-lung Lin (1999).
8. The fundamental challenge of nationalism to democratic stability comes from people's competing imaginations of the state's legitimate boundaries to which their nations should belong. If the people cannot form consensus on what the boundary of their state should be, hence want to join different states or create new independent

states, then it will be difficult, if not impossible, to generate a justifiable "majority rule" for democratic practices because the principle of majority rule presupposes the state being a consented unit. As Sir Ivor Jennings (1956: 56) remarked decades ago, " the people cannot decide until somebody decides who are the people." Dankwart Rustow(1970:350-2) explicitly treated "national unity" as a necessary background condition for democratic stability in his seminal work on democratic transitions, highlighting that democracy is a system of rule by temporary majorities, and for rulers and policies to be changed freely, the boundaries must endure and the composition of the citizenry be continuous. And according to Juan Linz and Alfred Stepan (1966: 1), democracy requires statehood; without a sovereign state, there can be no secure democracy. Simply put, *no state, no democracy.*

While no democracy can be fully consolidated without a clearly defined state boundary, it is not necessary for every consolidated democracy to be a nation-state. More specifically, the minimum requirement of a consolidated democracy is a basic consensus among the people on the legitimate boundary of their state, not the necessary congruence of the imagine nation and the territorial state. In fact, the calling for the merge of national identity and political state, i.e., the building of nation-states, is exactly why democratic consolidation has been so difficult in many multi-ethnic, multi-racial, or multi-national countries.

9. For details of the argument in this section, see Chia-lung Lin and Yun-han Chu (2000) and Chia-ling Lin (1999; 2000). On importance of political factors in explaining the development of nationalism, see Paul Brass (1991), John Breuilly (1993), Mark Thompson (1993), Rogers Brubaker (1996), Juan Linz and Alfred Stepan (1996).

10. Bruce Cumings (1984).

11. Edwin Winclker (1992).

12. See John Hutchinson and Anthony Smith, eds. (1994: 17-8).

13. By state-nation, Juan Linz (1993:2) refers to a strong sense of political loyalty endowed by citizens of multi-national or multi-cultural states that proponents of homogeneous nation-states perceive only nation-states can engender.

14. For details, see Chia-lung Lin (1998: 541-50).

15. For details, see Chia-lung Lin (1998: 522-4).

16. According to my interviews with hundreds of national and local politicians in Taiwan, many mentioned that the people of Taiwan and of the Mainland have developed two distinct sets of political culture. To them, the Chinese culture is in essence a continental culture, one that is agriculture-based and relative closed and conservative. On the contrary, Taiwan has developed an oceanic culture, which is trade-based and quite open, inclusive and multi-dimensional. The cultural differences across the Taiwan Strait have both political and social aspects. Politically, the Mainland people have a strong "Great China Complex," which encourages ethnocentrism as well as the worshiping of state authority and shows less respect for human rights, the rule of law, and democratic values. Socially speaking, decades of communist rule seem to have somewhat deprived the Mainland people of their sense of morality, making them more aggressive, bully and calculating, and lack of strong family values and sincere friendships.

17. For details of the argument, see Chia-lung Lin (1989).

18. In an interview with the author on October 19, 1998 Lee Teng-hui mentioned that

he had been concerned about the definition of the cross-strait relations ever since the National Affairs Conference ended and felt that he needed to have a new framework for handling cross-strait disputes. And the main purpose of setting up the National Unification Council and issuing the National Unification Guidelines was to prevent development in cross-strait relations and disputes on unification vs. independence from hindering Taiwan's democratization progress.

19.   For elaboration on Robert Putnam's two-level-game framework and its applications, see Peter Evens, Harold Jacobson and Robert Putnam, eds. (1993).

20.   For analyses on the strategic voting of Taiwanese voters, see Leonard Wantchekon and David Lam (1996) and Chia-lung Lin (1998: Chapter 10).

21.   For the U.S.'s difficulties in maintaining its "strategic ambiguity" policy after the drastic political change took place at both sides of the Taiwan Strait, see The-yu Wang (1996).

22.   Based on the author's interview with Lee Teng-hui.

23.   As Hsu Hui-you, Secretary General of the Association for Relations across the Taiwan Strait, revealed after President Lee mentioned the two-state theory, Lee actually considered enunciating his two-state theory as early as April of 1999, but had to delay it for various reasons (*United Daily*, August 22, 1999).

4 The Republic of China on Taiwan's "Pragmatic Diplomacy"

BRUCE J. DICKSON

Taiwan's diplomatic isolation is an anomaly. Although it ranks third in the world in total foreign exchange reserves, seventh in foreign trade, is a major provider of foreign aid, and is a textbook example of rapid and equitable economic development and a peaceful and incremental transition to democratization, it is all but excluded from the traditional forums of diplomacy. It has formal diplomatic ties with less than 30 countries, none of them significant players in the international community, and is excluded from most international governmental organizations, including the United Nations and its affiliated organizations, the World Bank, the International Monetary Fund, and even many regional forums in Asia. This gap between Taiwan's record of economic and political progress, on the one hand, and its international stature, on the other, is the result of the long struggle for international recognition and legitimization between the Republic of China on Taiwan and the People's Republic of China.

Domestic political change in Taiwan and the changing international environment have led Taiwan's leaders to embark on new initiatives to break out of its diplomatic isolation. For the past decade, the government has pursued "pragmatic diplomacy," recognizing the deterioration of its formal diplomatic recognition and also attempting to raise its international visibility.

Taiwan's pragmatic diplomacy has created an unusual type of security dilemma: its efforts to enhance its security by expanding its range of contacts with foreign countries and international organizations have led to sharp reactions from China which in fact have reduced its security. Domestic pressures to increase the international space in which Taiwan can operate, officially or unofficially, have been confronted with China's opposition to these efforts, leading to pressure on Taiwan and the countries and organizations with which it seeks to interact. Indeed, the bigger the prize, the bigger the price. The higher the profile of Taiwan's initiatives, and the higher the potential rewards if its efforts bear fruit, the stronger China's reaction, particularly when the United States is involved. Consequently, although pragmatic diplomacy is designed to regain some of the international recognition and respect its leaders and citizens feel they deserve, it has had the unintended consequence of imperiling its national security interests.

This chapter will begin with an overview of Taiwan's foreign policy strategy and the reasons why that strategy changed in the late 1980s, and discuss the key components of pragmatic diplomacy and its achievements, and assess its future challenges. Although cross-straits relations will not be discussed in any detail, Taiwan's relations with the mainland cannot fully be separated from any discussion of its foreign relations more generally. The motivations, goals, and limitations to Taiwan's pragmatic diplomacy are all directly related to China, and this will be a recurring theme. But it is Taiwan's initiatives that will be the focus.

I. Taiwan's Changing Diplomatic Strategy

Taiwan's current diplomatic isolation is in large part the result of past decisions by its leaders.[1] After its retreat to Taiwan in 1949, the ROC government rigidly abided by its claim to be the sole legitimate government of all of China, including the mainland, and did not accept dual recognition or joint membership in international organizations with the PRC. During the 1950s and 1960s, the ROC's diplomatic standing remained high because the Cold War precluded non-communist countries from developing formal ties with the PRC. This gave Taiwan strategic benefits: it had formal relations with most countries in the world and represented China in international organizations such as the United Nations, the World Bank, and the IMF. But as China emerged from its diplomatic isolation after the Cultural Revolution, and was seen by many countries, including the U.S., as an important counterweight to the Soviet Union, Taiwan's strategic value to the international community deteriorated. Beginning in the early 1970s, Canada, Japan, and a host of other countries established formal relations with the PRC, the PRC replaced the ROC as China's representative in most international organizations, and the U.S. gradually expanded its ties with the PRC, culminating in the establishment of formal diplomatic ties in 1979. Throughout the 1970s, the ROC lost diplomatic ties with 45 countries, reaching a low of 22 in 1978. During that same time, the PRC established ties with 70 countries, reaching a total of 117 by 1979. During these years, the two sides waged a zero-sum struggle for diplomatic recognition and refused to accept dual recognition because, as Samuel Kim noted, "each party came to view its own legitimation as dependent on the delegitimation of the other party."[2]

This declining diplomatic support, however, was not enough to change the ROC's adherence to its one China policy. It broke relations with countries that were about to establish ties with Beijing, and withdrew from the U.N. before the vote to expel it. This consistent behavior may have allowed it to save face and maintain internal legitimacy behind its claim to be the government of all China and thereby forestall demands for domestic political change that began to rise as its diplomatic standing fell, but its inflexible response to the changing international environment served to undermine its international support. Forced to choose between China and Taiwan, most countries and international organizations quite willingly chose the former. Taiwan's diplomatic isolation was largely self-inflicted.

Domestic political change gradually led to greater flexibility in Taiwan's foreign policy. Two related processes were at work. First, the original generation of mainlander elites, who had accompanied Chiang Kai-shek to Taiwan in 1949, were replaced by a new generation of leaders comprised of second-generation mainlanders and native Taiwanese. This younger generation of leaders was generally less motivated by the KMT's traditional ideology and goals, particularly unification with the mainland, and more focused on the developmental needs of Taiwan. In contrast to the generation of revolutionary mainlanders, they tended to be less dogmatic in their beliefs and more willing to adjust their policies in light of changing domestic and international environments.[3]

The second domestic change, partially a result of the generational change occurring within the KMT, was the growing support for the political opposition to the KMT and the emergence of a distinctly Taiwanese national identity. The political opposition, first the loosely organized *tangwai* and later the Democratic Progressive Party (DPP), was able to capitalize on public concern over Taiwan's diplomatic decline and the perception that the KMT did not represent the interests of Taiwan's citizens. Although there was (and remains) limited support for the DPP's goal of formal independence for Taiwan, it was able to tap into public discontent over the lack of international recognition enjoyed by Taiwan and lack of appreciation for its political and economic developments. Faced with these domestic pressures to increase

Taiwan's international stature, the government's traditionally inflexible foreign policy posture was increasingly untenable.

These international and domestic factors led to the adoption of "pragmatic diplomacy" in the late 1980s. This change in foreign policy strategy, not coincidentally, accompanied Lee Teng-hui's emergence as KMT chairman and ROC president. The content of this pragmatic diplomacy has three dimensions. First, it is designed to consolidate and strengthen Taiwan's existing formal diplomatic relations and develop new ones. Second, it is designed to develop and upgrade "substantive relations" with those countries Taiwan does not have formal ties. In this regard, it attempts to expand its trade and economic relations, cultural exchanges, and formal and informal political dialogs. Third, Taiwan seeks to participate or resume participation in a broad range of international organizations, both governmental and non-governmental. In contrast to the rigid and unimaginative diplomatic stance of the past, the new pragmatic diplomacy is designed to raise Taiwan's international profile in a variety of ways. Unfortunately, Taiwan's international standing is not solely of its own choosing. In all three of these areas, progress has been hampered not so much by the lack of international support or sympathy but by China's resistance. Taiwan's flexibility in its foreign relations has not been matched by similar changes in China's policy toward Taiwan's international status. In the following sections, trends in each of these areas will be assessed.

II. Maintaining and Expanding Diplomatic Ties

Taiwan currently has formal diplomatic ties with roughly 30 countries, concentrated in Central America, the Caribbean, Africa, the Pacific Islands, and also the Vatican. It actively courts these countries to maintain the relationships, offering them generous amounts of aid, loans, and investment, so much so that the PRC and even some critics in Taiwan have labeled these efforts as "dollar diplomacy." For example, the establishment of formal relations with Macedonia in 1998 was followed by a package of almost $400 million in loans and aid over two to five years. But China itself tries to entice these countries with promises of loans and aid to switch their diplomatic ties to Beijing, and Taiwan cannot afford to take them for granted. For instance, in January 1998, the Central African Republic switched its ties to Beijing, the third time since 1964 that it severed relations with Taiwan. For countries in dire economic straits, the competition between China and Taiwan for diplomatic recognition offers the opportunity to sell their embassy to the highest bidder.

Recent trends in Taiwan's relationships with Central American and Caribbean nations exemplify its efforts to maintain existing ties. In July 1997, Foreign Minister John Chang spent three weeks in the region, and offered $20 million in aid to six countries. In September, President Lee Teng-hui and six cabinet ministers spent two weeks in Central and South America, including a summit meeting with all Central American leaders. Lee pledged $56 million for an industrial development zone in Panama, $10 million in soft loans to businessmen in Panama, an unspecified amount for the maintenance of the canal; $15 million for an industrial development zone in Honduras; $10 million in low interest loans to both Panama and Honduras; and $20 million in loans to Paraguay. Taiwan joined the System of Central American Integration, a plan for economic and political integration in the region, including plans for a free trade zone, and pledged to capitalize 80% of a $240 Central American Development Fund. In June 1999, Taiwan committed $10 billion in cooperation and investment funds for Central America over the next ten years. Such support is greatly appreciated in these countries, which face a variety of economic woes. Chen Shui-bian's first diplomatic trip as president began in Central America. Although no new pledges of financial support were made during his trip, Chen reemphasized the importance of Taiwan's formal diplomatic partners.

The ROC government also encourages private enterprises to invest in the region. It pressured the Chinatrust Commercial Bank, Taiwan's largest private bank, and the International Commercial Bank of China to open branches in Paraguay and Panama, respectively. The rationale is that these banks are needed to funnel investment from Taiwan and service the activities of Taiwanese businessmen in the area, but the banks see them as unlikely to be profitable and are only complying with the government's request in the expectation of creating good will for the future. In addition to direct pressure, the government also offers inducements. In 1997, the Ministry of Economic Affairs announced it would provide 20% subsidies to new business ventures in countries that have formal diplomatic ties with Taiwan, with the remaining 80% eligible for low interest loans from the Export-Import Bank. The government is also willing to pay the travel expenses of businessmen traveling to Central America. This is all in keeping with Taiwan's traditional economic development strategy of providing state leadership to the private sector. But the private sector is not rushing to follow the government's lead. Even large companies such as Evergreen, which already has a large stake in Panama and elsewhere in the region, have been reluctant to cooperate with these new government initiatives because they are concerned it may jeopardize their expansion into the China market.[4]

To facilitate the maintenance and expansion of its formal ties, Taiwan no longer insists that other countries accept its version of the "one China" policy and may be willing to allow dual recognition. However, Beijing still does not accept such an arrangement. There was some conjecture that South Africa would be the first country to attempt dual recognition, but in the end it too was forced to choose. Ironically, on December 31, 1997, the day before South Africa opened its embassy in Beijing, Taipei severed its diplomatic ties with South Africa. Given Taipei's current willingness to accept dual recognition, it is unusual that Taiwan initiated the severing of ties.

III. Expanding Substantive Relations

The changing number of Taiwan's formal ties is a poor measure of its international standing. It also maintains extensive economic, cultural, and political relationships with a host of other countries. As of 2000, Taiwan had 97 representative offices in 63 countries with which it did not have formal ties. These institutions allow it to retain a presence and a degree of influence in the setting of those countries' policies toward China and Taiwan. They also allow Taiwan to offer regular consular functions, such as issuing visas and intervening on behalf of Taiwanese businessmen and tourists when they encounter difficulties. This was one of the primary motivations behind pragmatic diplomacy: not only was Taiwan not sufficiently integrated into the global community, it could not represent or defend its own citizens abroad.

However, China's concern that these substantive ties are part of a strategy to promote "creeping independence" for Taiwan have led it to be sensitive to the development and improvement of these unofficial ties. It frequently punishes countries that transgress what China believes to be appropriate interactions, and also periodically forces its diplomatic partners to reiterate their commitment to China's definition of the "one China" policy. Although it is willing to overlook visits by presidents and prime ministers from third world countries, it is acutely sensitive to Taiwan's improved relations with industrialized countries, and particularly the U.S.[5] The more prominent the country, the harsher is China's reactions. Within these constraints, Taiwan attempts to promote its pragmatic diplomacy, but progress has been episodic, limited, and occasionally costly.

To facilitate pragmatic diplomacy in the economic realm, Taiwan established a $1.1 billion International Economic Cooperation and Development Fund. From this fund, it provided loans to Vietnam, Belarus, and South Africa in 1992 for $8-15 million each. The six-year National Development Plan of $300 announced in 1991 (later scaled back by about one-fourth) included a large portion set aside for foreign contracts. It saw a window of opportunity in the collapse of communism in Eastern Europe and the former Soviet Union, opening trade offices in Latvia, Lithuania, Estonia, Russia, Hungary, the Czech Republic, and elsewhere. In 1991, it provided humanitarian food aid to Russia, Ukraine, and Belarus. It has also established government to government relations with many former communist countries, although short of full diplomatic relations. Latvia initially established consular relations with Taiwan but broke them off in 1994 under pressure from China. Taiwan's volume of total foreign trade, overseas investment, and foreign exchange reserves have continued to grow despite its diplomatic isolation.

Increased trade and investment are the most tangible aspect of its substantive relations, but Taiwan also has expanded ministerial-level contacts with a wide variety of countries. With the end of the Cold War, China's value as a strategic counterweight evaporated, and European countries in particular became more willing to expand unofficial ties with Taiwan.[6] These ties give its diplomacy a degree of officiality that is otherwise lacking, given its diplomatic isolation. In recent years, government officials from Taiwan have visited a variety of European, Asian, and North and South American countries. In addition, numerous top level officials have visited Taiwan, including Malaysian president Mahathir, Premier Lee Kuan Yew of Singapore, and cabinet level ministers from Europe and the United States. These visits are not designed to lead to formal diplomatic ties, but to enhance Taiwan's visibility in the international arena.

A. Relations with Southeast Asia

Taiwan has devoted considerable effort to developing its relations with its neighbors in Southeast Asia, for two reasons. The first is simply proximity: Taiwan shares similar security and economic concerns with the rest of Southeast Asia and seeks to maintain good relations with them. The second is related to China: Taiwan would like to have the support of Southeast Asian countries as a buffer against Chinese political and military pressure and as an alternative location for trade and investment. It has achieved clear but limited progress in both regards.

Southeast Asia has been the site of "vacation diplomacy" by Taiwan's leaders. Prime Minister Lien Chan vacationed in Singapore and Malaysia over the 1994 New Year's holiday, followed by Lee Teng-hui's vacation trips to the Philippines, Indonesia, and Thailand during the Chinese New Year in February 1994. Although these were billed as private vacations, the two leaders played golf with leaders in their host countries, met privately with other government leaders, and even had an audience with the Thai king and queen. In addition, it is an open secret that Singapore sends its soldiers to Taiwan for military training.

These trips were successful in forging closer ties with Taiwan's neighbors, but they did not have the full dividends that were hoped for. Under pressure from China, Taiwan remains excluded from the regional forums regarding security issues (such as the ASEAN Regional Forum and the Council for Security Cooperation in the Asia-Pacific [CSCAP]), although scholars from Taiwan have been invited to participate in its working group meetings.[7] Despite the warming of relations between Southeast Asia and Taiwan, most Asian leaders remained silent during the 1995-96 missile crises. The ASEAN countries are more concerned about China's actions in the South China Sea, but saw the Taiwan Straits crisis as an indication of the China's willingness to use military force to solve political problems. However, there were private communications of the concerns of the ASEAN countries and discussion of the matter at the Senior Officials Meeting in May 1996. Moreover, they also had "private approval but no public praise" for the U.S. decision to send the USS Nimitz through the Taiwan Straits in December 1995.[8]

Lee Teng-hui's "Go South" policy was designed to enhance Taiwan's economic ties with Southeast Asia, largely in order to reduce its dependency on trade and investment with China. More than most of Taiwan's other politicians and businessmen, Lee was alarmed by the increasing integration of the Taiwan's economy with the mainland and refused to drop remaining restrictions on direct trade and transportation across the straits. As an alternative, he promoted the "Go South" policy to promote business opportunities in Southeast Asia. Taiwan became the largest investor in Vietnam and a major source of investment for Malaysia, Thailand, Indonesia, and the Philippines. However, new investments in those countries declined in recent years, as private investors focused more and more on the potential of China market.[9] Instead, it was government and KMT owned enterprises which took the leading role in signing new contracts for projects in Southeast Asia.[10]

Taiwan saw an opportunity for strategic and diplomatic gains from the East Asian financial crisis that began in 1997. Vice President Lien Chan, Prime Minister Vincent Siew, and other delegations of government officials and leading businessmen made several trips throughout the region in 1998. However, offers of aid and relief met with a variety of obstacles. China accused Taiwan of using the crisis for its own political gains. Zhu Rongji even criticized Taiwan's decision to devalue its currency, which could have exacerbated the financial crisis, in order to draw attention to Beijing's decision to maintain its exchange rate and to undermine support for Taiwan's offers of assistance. The government's proposed multi-billion dollar bailout of South Korea met with a storm of protest in Taiwan: the proposed amount was not enough to make a difference, and there is still resentment about how South Korea broke relations in 1991 without warning and has remained distant since.

Without diplomatic ties or membership in the IMF, how to transmit official aid was also a problem.[11] In January 1998, Siew made separate trips to the Philippines and Indonesia to assess the financial crisis and discuss Taiwan's role in their recovery. The KMT established a new holding capitalized at $625 million to invest in Southeast Asian stock markets.[12] Private investment is the preferred option, but many businessmen were still skeptical about the financial soundness of new investments in countries that were still sinking under financial and economic problems. As in Central America, many businessmen are unwilling to follow the government's lead unless it makes good business sense.[13] When it does make sense, though, they are willing to commit. For example, following Siew's trip to Malaysia in April 1998, several Taiwanese companies signed investment deals, ranging from real estate to information technology.

B. Relations with the United States

The key to Taiwan's pragmatic diplomacy -- and to its security dilemma -- is its relations with the United States. Although formal ties were ended in 1979, the U.S. and Taiwan continue to maintain a full array of political, economic, security, and cultural relationships. These ties are guided in part by the Taiwan Relations Act of 1979, but more fundamentally by the history of the relationship itself and the commitment of administrations of both parties throughout the post-war period. Taiwan's current status as a political entity independent of the PRC's direct control is made possible only by the implicit American commitment to Taiwan's security.

The U.S. has long been Taiwan's leading trade partner, but even this has been a source of contention. Taiwan runs a large annual trade surplus with the U.S., which peaked at $16 billion in 1987. Since then, Taiwan has sent regular "buy American" trade delegations to the U.S. to bring down the surplus and to maintain political support. It has frequently been punished for unfair or illegal trade practices, including intellectual property rights violations, limited access to Taiwan's financial and services sectors, dumping, and trading in endangered species. In contrast to China, however, Taiwan has generally made good progress in resolving these disputes, although the threat and sometimes the imposition of sanctions is normally required for its compliance. It also lobbies extensively in Congress, directly by representatives from Taiwan's ersatz embassy in the U.S., the Taipei Economic and Cultural Representative Office (TECRO) and indirectly through such groups as Formosan Association for Public Affairs (FAPA) and the Cassidy and Associates consulting firm. This diversity of voices speaking on behalf of Taiwan often makes it difficult to maintain a clear and consistent message. Taiwan also hosts numerous delegations of Congressmen and their staffers each year to build good will.

Lee Teng-hui's trip to Cornell in May 1995 was the crowning achievement of his pragmatic diplomacy strategy and also the epitome of the security dilemma inherent in that strategy. Beijing responded to this unofficial trip with vehemence: it broke off scheduled negotiations between Taiwan's Straits Exchange Foundation and China's Association for Relations Across the Taiwan Straits (the two nominally private organizations responsible for direct contacts between the governments in China and Taiwan), withdrew its ambassador to the U.S., canceled a scheduled visit by its defense minister to the U.S., began an increasingly bitter rhetorical attack on Taiwan and Lee personally, and within months began two episodes of military exercises in the region, including the launching of live missiles off Taiwan's coasts. The vehemence of China's reaction was unanticipated in both Washington and Taipei, and required almost two years to restore the status quo ante.

In Taiwan, although Lee's approval ratings quickly rebounded after an initial decline and he went on to win the presidential election by a landslide in the wake of the missile crisis, he was criticized for being reckless and using his Cornell trip to bolster his presidential prospects at the expense of Taiwan's security. Lee retreated from such high profile trips. After his election, he announced he was too busy to accept an invitation to travel again to the U.S. and speak to Congress, and it was almost two years before his next foreign trip, this time to Central America (described above). During Lee's second term in office, he took no "private" trips to countries with whom Taiwan did not have formal diplomatic ties. Never the less, popular support for pragmatic diplomacy remained high in Taiwan and the vast majority believed Lee's trips abroad helped Taiwan, ranging from 85% for Lee's Cornell trip to 66% for his 1997 trip to Central America.[14] And according to a September 1997 poll by the Center for Public Opinion and Election Studies, National Sun Yat-sen University, 71% of Taiwanese support developing foreign ties even if it led to rising tensions with China.[15]

In the U.S., the administration and Congress represent alternative viewpoints on the proper nature of U.S.-Taiwan relations and their implications for U.S.-China relations. The administration has been reluctant to raise the level of unofficial relations beyond cosmetic changes, most notably the renaming of the Taiwan's office in the U.S. as the Taipei Economic and Cultural Representative Office (formerly the non-descript Coordination Council for North American Activities). Certain cabinet level exchanges are permissible, although the presence of a representative from the American Institute in Taiwan[16] is often required to maintain the appearance of a private meeting. The principals of the national security team (president, vice president, secretaries of state and defense, and national security advisor, as well as their counterparts in Taiwan) are prevented by precedent (not by law) from meeting each other. However, Taiwan's leaders have been granted permission to make brief stop-overs in the U.S. on their way to or from foreign countries. In general, the administrative branch is more concerned with upholding the commitments to the one China policy, as expressed in the three U.S.-China communiques of 1972, 1979, and 1982, than in risking that relationship by promoting closer political ties with Taiwan.

Taiwan receives more support in Congress. Much of this support is symbolic: Taiwan represents the commitment to a free market economy and progress toward democratization, and it offers a sharp contrast with the current reality in China. Taiwan benefits from the strong anti-China sentiments among many members of Congress. However, many of Taiwan's supporters in Congress are ignorant of the complex interactions between the U.S., China, and Taiwan. In 1995, as China was retaliating against the issuance of a visa to Lee Teng-hui, Newt Gingrich said the U.S. should simply go ahead and recognize Taiwan's independence and wait for China to eventually get over it. He later retracted that statement, undoubtedly at the urging of Taiwan's diplomats, because his proposal was inconsistent with Taiwan's current policy. Such views may be well intentioned, but also reflect how uninformed support for Taiwan threatens to undermine its security rather than enhance it. In 2000, the House of Representatives passed the "Taiwan Security Enhancement Act" with overwhelming, bipartisan support. This bill would mandate closer military interaction between the U.S. and Taiwan than has been the case for several decades, which would likely infuriate China and lead to a huge setback in the overall relationship between the U.S. and China.[17] Unlike the White House, Congress is unwilling to preserve U.S.-China relations at the expense of the American relationship with Taiwan.

Outside of government, most discussions of the "Taiwan issue" take unification as the assumed end-point. Many China specialists express a degree of resentment at Taiwan's actions in promoting pragmatic diplomacy when those actions damage U.S.-China relations and lead to the prospect of direct conflict. Proposals to maintain the status quo are often motivated by the assumption that after a certain period of time conditions for a negotiated process leading to unification will be more promising; the goal in the meantime is to keep Taiwan from upsetting the status quo so much that China is compelled to retaliate.[18] There is little discussion of how to make China more flexible, more willing to grant Taiwan some additional international space, or more accepting of Taiwan's claim that after decades of separation, Beijing does not exercise sovereign control over Taiwan. And while there is general support for Taiwan among the American public more generally, most Americans are unaware of the specifics of Taiwan's case and may not be willing to commit American troops to its defense.[19]

In the past, the U.S. was confronted with a difficult dilemma in its relations with China and Taiwan: how to commit to Taiwan's security enough to deter China's use of force against Taiwan without making Taiwan's leaders so confident of American support that they felt they had a blank check to do whatever they liked. This led to the policy commonly referred to as "strategic ambiguity": the U.S. would not commit itself publicly to a future course of action, but by implication it would defend Taiwan against an unprovoked attack from the mainland, but not against an attack precipitated by a unilateral declaration of independence by Taiwan. The U.S. is unwilling to be more specific, recognizing that Taiwan was unlikely to be satisfied with anything short of a blanket guarantee of its security and China was unlikely to be satisfied with any pledge of American involvement in what Beijing regards as its internal affairs. Administration leaders of both parties have defended this policy, arguing that the ambiguity has maintained peace and security in the Taiwan Straits and has fostered improved ties between China and Taiwan, especially in the economic realm.

Following Lee's visit to Cornell and subsequent tensions with China, the dilemma of U.S. relations with Taiwan and China evolved into a more concrete (although still not formally articulated) policy. The U.S. resolve to defend Taiwan from an unprovoked assault from China was made apparent during the March 1996 missile crisis in the Taiwan Straits, when the U.S. sent two aircraft carrier fleets to the area to show its concern that the conflict not escalate beyond the firing of live missiles off the northern and southern coasts of Taiwan. This unprecedented step was a clear signal of American support for Taiwan, and reportedly infuriated China's military and civilian leaders.

The second dimension of the strategic ambiguous policy (regarding a limited commitment to Taiwan's defense) has so far been made only indirectly by former officials. In early 1998, a high powered delegation led by former secretary of defense William Perry, former chairman of the Joint Chiefs of Staff John Shalikashvili, former national security advisor Brent Scowcroft, and former assistant secretary of defense for international security policy Ashton Carter traveled to Taipei to convey the message to both the KMT and DPP that they should not depend on American support if Taiwan declared independence.[20] The U.S. was not likely to recognize its independence nor commit its soldiers to Taiwan's defense in such an event. An earlier trip by former undersecretary of defense Joseph Nye and a subsequent trip by former national security advisor Anthony Lake conveyed the same message.[21] These trips by former officials from both Democratic and Republican administrations were designed to say what incumbent officials could not: that the American commitment to Taiwan's security is resolute and credible, but not open-ended. After Chen Shui-bian's victory in the presidential election of 2000, President Clinton and other government spokesmen immediately reconfirmed their commitment to the "one China" principle, making clear the limits on U.S. support for Taiwan.

The new clarity of U.S. policy is motivated by two factors. First, the desire to maintain the general improvement of U.S.-China relations is pushing American policy makers to preempt another conflict over Taiwan that could imperil that relationship. Second, the DPP was improving its performance in elections, first in the county level elections of 1997 in which it won a majority of the administrative posts, and Chen Shui-bian's dramatic victory in the presidential election of 2000. The DPP's charter includes support for Taiwan's formal independence, raising concerns that a DPP administration would provoke a conflict with China that would inevitably draw in the U.S. Although the DPP is rhetorically committed to the independence of Taiwan, some in the party, including Chen Shui-bian, have tried to soften the DPP's pledge to pursue independence, recognizing that this prospect is frightening to most voters in Taiwan, as it is alarming to policy makers in China and the U.S. Moderates in the DPP want to demonstrate that they can be trusted not to threaten Taiwan's security by recklessly promoting Taiwan's independence. The U.S. has been using private channels of communication to make clear to both the KMT and DPP that it will not recognize a declaration of independence, nor defend it against a use of force by China in that context. After Chen's victory, the U.S. sent a series of envoys to Taiwan to reiterate the American desire for the maintenance of peace in the Taiwan Straits.

In addition, the U.S. has quietly been encouraging China and Taiwan to reopen direct communications as a way to lessen tensions and improve relations on all three of the U.S.-China-Taiwan triangle. This is one way to mitigate Taiwan's security dilemma: by using official and quasi-official institutions to make its intentions transparent to China. The U.S. has been willing to encourage and support this effort by using unofficial delegations and other private channels of communication to provide information to both sides. So-called "track two" meetings have occurred in D.C. and New York with growing frequency in recent years. These meetings allow policy advisors, scholars, and even government officials from the U.S., China, and Taiwan to meet and exchange views, although little tangible progress is apparent so far. However, the U.S. is not willing to act as a formal mediator, as it has done in the Middle East or in the former Yugoslavia.

IV. Participation in International Organizations

The third dimension of Taiwan's pragmatic diplomacy is to increase the number of international organizations in which it is able to participate. Taiwan is currently excluded from the most prominent and influential international organizations, including the United Nations, the World Bank, IMF, Interpol, and others. Even where it is allowed to participate, its title and level of representation are often circumscribed by Chinese pressure on other members.

In order to participate in international organizations, Taiwan has been forced to relinquish many of the symbols of sovereignty. It cannot use its formal name, the Republic of China on Taiwan, nor its flag. Instead, it has had to accept titles such as "Taipei, China" or "Chinese Taipei" and its athletes in the Olympics fly the Olympic flag rather than the ROC flag. These compromises have been necessary to allow Taiwan's participation. In addition, its leaders are not able to attend certain activities of international organizations even when it is a member. In 1994, Japan was forced to withdraw its invitation to Lee Teng-hui to attend the Asian Games; instead vice president Hsu Li-teh went in an unofficial capacity. Lee has also not been invited to attend the APEC summit meetings, even though Taiwan is a full member. One of the primary goals of Lee's and Lien Chan's trips to Southeast Asia in 1993 was to secure an invitation to the 1994 APEC meetings in Bali, but in the end he was not invited, nor was he invited to subsequent meetings. Instead, Taiwan has had to settle for informal representation to the APEC meetings.

In 1991, Taiwan abandoned its claim to represent all of China, and announced a new claim of sovereignty that is limited to the territory it currently occupies, the island of Taiwan and several small islands off the coast of China. In that capacity, it has been trying to join or rejoin several international organizations. In September 1992, Taiwan received observer status in the GATT as the "customs territory of Taiwan, Penghu, Kinmen, and Matsu" and it is later applied to join the World Trade Organization under that designation. Its accession to the WTO was hampered by negotiations with member states regarding market access and more importantly by

China's insistence that it be admitted before Taiwan.

Taiwan's quixotic bid to join the United Nations exemplifies the challenges it faces in increasing its participation in international organizations. Under pressure from the DPP, the KMT government began its campaign to join the United Nations under a "divided state" formula, which had been used by Germany and Korea in the past to gain dual representation in the U.N. During his confirmation hearings in 1993, prime minister designate Lien Chan said he supported dual recognition of China and Taiwan and Taiwan's entry into the U.N.[22] In 1993, 23 nations, all with formal ties with Taiwan, endorsed the proposal in the General Assembly, but China was able to keep the item off the agenda. In subsequent years, the number of countries endorsing the proposal has increased slightly, but still without success. Due to China's absolute refusal to consider the proposal, no major country has been willing to endorse or even provide moral support to Taiwan's bid. The European Parliament passed a resolution supporting Taiwan's admission to international organizations and urged the United Nations to create a task force to study the feasibility of Taiwan's participation in U.N.-affiliated organizations, and the U.S. House of Representatives endorsed this resolution, but the governments of the countries involved have not wanted to take up the cause.[23]

The U.S. has stated repeatedly that it will not endorse Taiwan's bid because it would violate the "one China" policy. In particular, the U.S. will not support Taiwan's membership in international organizations that require sovereignty as a condition of membership. Such organizations include the United Nations, the World Bank, the International Monetary Fund, and their affiliated agencies, such as the World Health Organization. The U.S. has said it would support Taiwan's membership in organizations where statehood is not a requirement, and would support opportunities for Taiwan's voice to be heard in organizations where it is not a member,[24] but in practice the U.S. has done little to allow Taiwan's perspective to be heard in such bodies. President Bill Clinton reiterated that the U.S. would not support Taiwan's membership in organizations like the U.N. during his trip to China in 1998.[25] The U.S. is not willing to confront China on an unwinnable issue; with its possession of a veto in the Security Council, China is able to block the admission of any country into the U.N.

Although the bid to join the U.N. is widely seen as futile, the effort has several side benefits. For one thing, it is immensely popular among Taiwan's citizens. In a 1997 poll, almost 92% said they agreed or strongly agreed that Taiwan should join the U.N. The poll also revealed that respondents recognized it was China, not the international community, that was to blame for its continued exclusion: 80% said China was the main obstacle, and only 7% blamed lack of international support.[26] The U.N. bid also maintains momentum for Taiwan's claim for international recognition and keeps the issue on the international agenda. It is a reminder of China's intransigence on the issue and of the economic and political principles Taiwan represents that are more consistent with international norms than is China's behavior. As Michael Yahuda recently wrote, "Clearly it is more dangerous for the people of Taiwan to be ignored or overlooked than it is to be seen to be thwarted by China at the U.N... In practice, however, the ROCOT has made little progress."[27] Nor is it likely to in the foreseeable future. But the domestic and international benefits that accrue from the effort will likely keep it alive for the foreseeable future. Despite the low prospects for success, Chen Shui-bian restated his commitment to campaign for U.N. membership in the early months of his administration because the effort had such strong popular support among the people in Taiwan.

V. Conclusion

Taiwan's pragmatic diplomacy has achieved notable but limited success during recent years. But the success or failure of the policy is not determined by Taiwan's implementation but by China's resistance. The effort to create greater international space has made incremental progress, but the effects on Taiwan's security has been mixed. Each success has been matched by retaliation by China against both Taiwan and the nations with which it interacts. Like all security dilemmas, each effort to enhance Taiwan's security through pragmatic diplomacy carries the risk of undermining its security by antagonizing China. Is there a way out of this security dilemma?

International relations specialists would point to several possible solutions to the dilemma. First, the nation attempting to improve its security must convince its adversary that its actions are defensive, not offensive, in nature. This is normally proposed for arms build-ups, but has lessons for Taiwan's diplomatic efforts as well. If it could convince China that its new initiatives are designed to maintain its security and international standing in a dynamic world, but are not the early steps toward "creeping independence," then it might make more progress without incurring Beijing's wrath. But

China believes that Taiwan is trying to challenge, not defend, the status quo, and therefore its pragmatic diplomacy is "offensive" not defensive in nature. In this regard, Beijing's mistrust of Taiwan's goals inhibit communication and understanding.

Institutionalists would offer a related proposal: to establish and utilize institutions to make Taiwan's means and ends more transparent and therefore less threatening to China. Such institutions currently exist (the Straits Exchange Foundation on the Taiwan side and the Association for Relations Across the Taiwan Straits on the China side), but have had limited impact so far. Such institutions can only operate effectively when they are used to channel information between the two sides and when they share similar objectives. That has not yet been the case. Direct communication has been sporadic and susceptible to political interruptions, such as following Lee Teng-hui's trip to Cornell in 1995 and his 1999 declaration that relations between China and Taiwan should be conducted on the basis of "special state to state relations." The proper institutions exist, but have not yet been used to their full potential.

Finally, the security dilemma can be mitigated by the involvement of a third party as mediator or conciliator. Singapore has played this role to an extent, hosting the Koo-Wang Talks in 1994, but does not have leverage over either side to impose or enforce an agreement. More important, Lee Kuan Yew has been critical of Lee Teng-hui's promotion of Taiwanese identify and distancing Taiwan from China. His advice to Chen and other new leaders in Taiwan is to recognize that unification is the best and only solution to the problem of peace and security in the region.[28] The U.S. has been unwilling to broker a deal the way it did in the Middle East, the former Yugoslavia, or Northern Ireland, but as noted above has used unofficial delegations to encourage the two sides to resume negotiations on their own terms.

Changes in Taiwan's domestic politics and in the international environment will continue to provide momentum for its pragmatic diplomacy, but so long as China does not adjust its policies toward the Taiwan issue, progress toward increasing Taiwan's international standing and enhancing its security will be incremental at best.

Notes

1.   For useful overviews of Taiwan's diplomatic history, see Michael Ying-mao Kau, "The ROC's New Foreign Policy Strategy," in Denis Fred Simon and Michael Y.M. Kau, eds., *Taiwan: Beyond the Economic Miracle* (M.E. Sharpe, 1992), pp. 237-55; Samuel S. Kim, "Taiwan and the International System: The Challenge of Legitimization," in Robert Sutter and William Johnson, eds., *Taiwan in World Affairs* (Westview, 1993), pp. 145-89; and Chiao Chiao Hsieh, "Pragmatic Diplomacy: Foreign Policy and Foreign Relations," in Peter Ferdinand, ed., *Take-off for Taiwan?* (London: Chatham House, 1997), pp. 66-76.

2.   Kim, "Taiwan and the International System," p. 149.

3.   Bruce J. Dickson, *Democratization in China and Taiwan: The Adaptability of Leninist Parties* (Oxford University Press, 1997), pp. 111-30.

4.   Julian Baum, "Let's Tango: Taipei Asks Investors to Back Its Diplomatic Goals," *Far Eastern Economic Review* (hereafter *FEER*), October 9, 1997, pp. 29-32.

5.   Kim, "Taiwan and the International System," p. 155.

6.   Hsieh, "Pragmatic Diplomacy," pp. 87-91.

7.   Cheng-yi Lin, "Taiwan's South China Sea Policy," *Asian Survey*, vol. 37, no. 4 (April 1997), p. 328.

8.   Allen S. Whiting, "ASEAN Eyes China: The Security Dimension," *Asian Survey*, vol. 37, no. 4 (April 1997), pp. 299-322.

9.   Yu-shan Wu, "Taiwan in 1994: Managing a Critical Relationship," *Asian Survey*, vol. 35, no. 1 (January 1995), pp. 61-69.

10.   Philip Liu, "Golf Ball Diplomacy," *Free China Review*, May 1994, pp. 30-37.

11.   This was also a problem for Taiwan's offer of aid to Kosovo in 1998, which was blocked by China. Lee Teng-hui pledged $300 million to relief efforts, but little of it was ever delivered.

12.   *FEER*, March 26, 1998, p. 71.

13.   Julian Baum, "A Friend in Need: Taiwan Seeks to Aid Neighbors, But Business Balks," *FEER*, January 22, 1998, p. 24.

14.   *Lianhebao*, September 20, 1997.

15.   Survey results provided by Mainland Affairs Commission.

16.   The American Institute in Taiwan is the quasi-official organization that handles the unofficial relations between the US and Taiwan. Its representative in Taiwan serves as the de facto US ambassador and the AIT offices handle all normal consular duties. To symbolize AIT's unofficial status, it is headquartered in Rosslyn, Virginia, just outside Washington, DC, although the head of AIT has frequent meetings and contacts with counter-parts in the White House, State Department, Pentagon, and other departments, and often testifies before Congress on US policy toward Taiwan.

17.   As of this writing (fall 2000), the Senate had no plans to vote on this bill, and it was unclear if the bill would be revived in a future session of Congress.

18.   For instance, Thomas Robinson recently wrote that "the American interest -- while certainly supportive of democracy on and free trade with the island -- is to get beyond the Taiwan problem and thus to persuade Taipei to make whatever viable settlement it can with Beijing sooner rather than later"; see his "America in Taiwan's

Post-Cold War Foreign Relations," *China Quarterly*, no. 148 (December 1996), p. 1342. Although this statement is blunter than most, it captures the general sentiment among many China specialists.

19.   "Poll Shows Lukewarm Support for US Security Assistance to Taiwan," *Central Daily News*, October 19, 1999.

20.   John Pomfret, "U.S. Seeks China-Taiwan Dialog: Delegation Attempts to Facilitate Back Channel of Communication," *Washington Post*, February 21, 1998, p. A16.

21.   Nye has proposed changing US policy on the Taiwan issue to forestall conflict. The US would state it would not recognize a declaration of independence or come to Taiwan's defense if it did so. He would not require China to renounce the use of force, although the US would repeat that it would not accept the use of force. However, he stops short of saying what the US would do in such an event. See his "A Taiwan Deal," *Washington Post*, March 8, 1998, p. C7. For an account of Lake's trip, see Julian Baum, "Strait Talking: Americans Prod Taipei and Beijing to Restart Talks," *FEER*, March 26, 1998, pp. 28-29.

22.   Kim, "Taiwan and the International System," p. 165.

23.   Dennis V. Hickey, "U.S. Policy and Taiwan's Bid to Rejoin the United Nations," *Asian Survey*, vol. 37, no. 1 (November 1997), pp. 1031-43.

24.   See Congressional testimony by Winston Lord, US Department of State Dispatch, October 17, 1994, p. 706.

25.   While in Shanghai, Clinton declared the so-called "three no's" policy: no support for Taiwan independence, no support for a "one China, one Taiwan" policy, and no support for Taiwan's membership in international organizations that require sovereignty as a requirement for membership. Although each of these elements of the policy had been stated before, Clinton's statement had a dramatic impact because it was made in China and was not accompanied by a parallel statement of continued American support for Taiwan. See Andrew J. Nathan, "What's Wrong with American Taiwan Policy," *Washington Quarterly*, Spring 2000.

26.   *Zhongyang ribao*, January 20, 1997.

27.   Michael Yahuda, "The International Standing of the Republic of China on Taiwan," *China Quarterly*, no. 148 (December 1996), p. 1337.

28.   See his interview in Far Eastern Economic Review, June 8, 2000, pp. 16-18.

5 Taiwan in APEC's Trade Structure: Deutsch and Hirshman Revisited

STEVE CHAN

I. Theoretical Motivations

Given its diplomatic isolation, trade plays an especially important part in Taiwan's external relations. Foreign commerce, as Karl Deutsch and his colleagues wrote over four decades ago, can help to foster "relative acceptance" and mutual responsiveness among nations.[1] Increasing commercial and noncommercial contact has the effect of deepening and widening networks of cross-national interests and institutions. These networks and shared norms underpin the rise of a "security community," whereby the idea of resorting to arms as a method of settling international disagreement becomes simply "unthinkable." Political, cultural, and economic exchanges (e.g., diplomatic consultation, foreign tourism and investment) all contribute to the process of integration and the promotion of nonviolent intercourse. Trade, however, seems to have been accorded a particularly prominent role in promoting peaceful international relations.

The proposition that trade can have a pacifying influence is certainly not new. For example, over two centuries ago Immanuel Kant commented that commerce contributes to a "cosmopolitan spirit."[2] This outlook, along with a republican form of government, encourages a respect for the rule of law both domestically and internationally. The consequent norm of liberal internationalism in turn was supposed to foster a security community of like-minded nations -- a "pacific union" that promises "perpetual peace."

Some recent theoretical and empirical works echo or confirm the importance of trade in promoting international peace. Financial and commercial issues rise to the top of policy agendas in a world of "complex interdependence."[3] The overt exercise or threat of military force becomes rare and even counter-productive in this world, whereas the acumen for forging cross-issue linkages and cross-national coalitions gains greater currency. Among those countries whose relations are characterized by dense webs of interlocking "low politics," the active participation of multiple cross-cutting interest groups in the policy process blurs the domains of domestic and international politics. The conduct and formulation of foreign policy become more constrained by the rise of domestic constituents with a vested interest in particular foreign policy issues. The necessity of "domestic ratification" gives rise to the conception of international relations as "two-level games"[4] -- a development that, according to the international liberals, should restrain the escalation of international conflict.

This restraining effect of domestic ratification derives in part from the Kantian supposition that the mass public is less disposed to war-making than their leaders. Sensing that they will have to assume the burden of war (in blood, sweat, tears, and dollars), voters are reluctant to initiate war. According to this logic, democracies -- where voters exercise sovereign power -- are more peaceful. More pertinent to the topic of this paper, the requirement of domestic ratification is also supposed to discourage foreign belligerence because vested commercial interests on both sides of a conflict have much to lose if their trade is jeopardized. This view suggests that the more active the ongoing commercial ties, the stronger will be the bilateral interests in maintaining these ties -- and the more likely that the parties will be self-motivated to resolve their differences peacefully. Recent studies by Oneal, Russett and their colleagues[5] tend to support both hypotheses just mentioned. They found that democratic systems of government and economic interdependence in trade have had significant and independent effects in dampening the incidence and escalation of international conflict.

Significantly, however, there is another side to the view that trade promotes peace and mutual gain. In his classic study published shortly after World War II, Albert Hirschman[6] wrote about the role of trade in economic statecraft. Trade is a double-edged sword. On the one hand, it can compensate for domestic scarcities and permit the more efficient allocation of production resources through the pursuit of national comparative advantage. On the other hand, it can trap a country in a dependency relationship, making it sensitive and/or vulnerable to foreign attempts at economic coercion. Trade, in other words, can be used by others as a leverage to gain political concessions.

Hirschman studied the strategic trade behavior of the major powers during the interwar years. One manifestation of this conduct was the deliberate attempt by these countries to orient their trade toward the smaller nations (small in terms of trade volume, not necessarily in physical size) -- thereby making themselves more influential trade partners for the latter. Conversely, an over-reliance on a few trade partners and/or commodities characterized the plight of the smaller countries, converting them into economic dependents of their larger counterparts. This phenomenon was most clearly exemplified in Nazi Germany's commercial relations with the Southeast European states.

Berlin's policy was to initially purchase Balkan exports, mostly agricultural and mineral products, at prices above the world market. This practice helped to foster dependency on the German market, which became more and more indispensable as a source of export revenue for the Balkan countries. Rising Balkan export dependency on Germany was followed by Berlin's own export drive to capture the Southeast European markets. Germany's exports were primarily manufactured products, thus creating a classic system of asymmetric trade relationships involving the exchange of Balkan raw materials for German industrial goods.

Asymmetric trade such as that just described became a familiar theme in the dependency literature.[7] Moreover, the proposition that foreign trade has important consequences for national power and autonomy has been the hallmark of mercantilist theorizing since at least the seminal work of Friedrich List.[8]   For both List and contemporary mercantilists (and *dependentistas*), foreign trade more often than not involves unequal exchanges which provide more relative gains for some than others. Moreover, economic power and political power are invariably intertwined and to a substantial extent fungible. Economic advantages offer one means to achieve political domination, and political influence in turn creates the basis for further economic exploitation.

Yet a fate of economic dependent and political pawn is not inevitable for all small countries.[9] Thus, for example, contrary to the experience of the Balkan countries, the Scandinavian and the Benelux countries did not succumb to Berlin's strategic trade. The latter countries' more developed economies and their more effective counter-measures helped to defuse Germany's trade offensive.[10]   More recently, the Asian tigers have been widely cited as prominent examples of economic upward mobility. Whether due to internal effort mobilization or skillful external negotiation,[11] the conventional wisdom has these newly industrializing economies (NIEs) overcoming serious handicaps in terms of meager physical endowment, unfavorable domestic carrying capacity, lateness in industrialization, and acute strategic vulnerability. Until the economic turmoil of late 1997, these economies appeared to have been consistent "overachievers" whose international economic status has experienced continuous ascendance.

II. Policy Predicaments

How does the preceding discussion relate to Asia Pacific generally and Taiwan particularly? Notwithstanding the recent economic difficulties of some of its constituent economies, Asia Pacific has been the most dynamic region of the world since World War II. It is also a region where multilateral institutions, notwithstanding recent meetings of APEC (Asia Pacific Economic Cooperation) leaders, have remained relatively weak, informal, and ad hoc. Bilateral relations with key foreign counterparts remain more important for most countries than multilateral institutions. Moreover, given the heavy trade orientation of the Asian countries, export success is important not only for reasons of economic well-being but also for those of regime legitimacy. In the absence of formal diplomatic relations, commercial ties acquire additional significance for Taiwan.

To what extent would trade and other forms of interaction with Mainland China help to defuse tension across the Taiwan Strait? That is, would Mainland China be self-deterred from undertaking confrontational policies that would disrupt the ongoing economic ties? Would these ongoing exchanges initiate a process that leads eventually to de facto integration if not de jure amalgamation? Conversely, would the rising volume of cross-Strait economic exchanges produce significant asymmetries such as those that characterized the German-Balkan relations prior to World War II, economic asymmetries that would in turn lead to political vulnerability and subjugation?

Japan and the U.S. also loom large in Taiwan's external relations. To the extent that trade with these countries fosters influential transnational coalitions with a vested interest in maintaining the political status quo, it redounds to Taipei's advantage even -- perhaps especially -- in the absence of formal diplomatic recognition. Domestic groups in Japan and the U.S. would be self-motivated to lobby their governments lest the status quo be compromised to their detriment or to the benefit of a competitor. Of course, as with any other country, excessive trade dependence on either Tokyo or Washington can become a source of political liability.

Diversification of trade partners helps to forestall asymmetric dependence and avoid putting one's political and economic eggs in one basket. The smaller APEC countries share this concern and have a common interest in engaging in multilateral efforts to lessen the liability of concentrating too much trade on one or two partners. To this end, they would have to do more business among themselves. They would have to export more to each other, and to import more from each other. However, quite aside from the constraint imposed by their limited absorptive capacity, these countries tend to be trade competitors. That is, they tend to push similar exports and demand similar imports. Accordingly, the smaller APEC countries face cross-pressure from their political and economic interests.

As implied above, Taiwan faces a series of predicaments. The heavy reliance of its exports on the U.S. and the chronic bilateral trade surplus favoring Taiwan have been a source of concern, and call for greater diversification of trade to other countries. Efforts in the latter direction, however, face structural impediments in the Japanese and European markets. Caught between the rising protectionism of the U.S. and the increasing competition from the other NIEs -- the so-called sandwich effect -- Taiwan's labor-intensive producers are inclined to look to Mainland China both as an export-platform and as an alternative market for their goods. While helping to give a new lease of life to such declining industries and while establishing new cross-Strait economic linkages, this move presents political risks. The double-edged nature of trade therefore requires efforts to finesse the various predicaments, so that one could make economic and political gains without having to incur the concomitant liabilities. For reasons already mentioned -- such as its diplomatic isolation, its export-oriented economy, and its contentious relationship with Mainland China -- this policy challenge is especially acute for Taiwan. This island's trade predicaments also help to bring into sharper focus the debate among the liberal, mercantilist, and dependency perspectives about the political consequences of external economic relations.

III. APEC Trade Structure

Several pervious papers[12] addressed APEC's evolving structure of economic exchanges. Using Hirschman's original indicators of trade concentration and product exchange, they concluded that the export and import patterns for the major APEC members departed significantly from mercantilist and dependency expectations. Contrary to the tendency observed by Hirschman among the major trade powers of the 1930s, U.S. imports from and exports to the other APEC partners were not tilted toward the smaller countries (again, smallness in this context refers to trade volume and not physical size). A bias toward trading with the smaller countries was an important part of Nazi Germany's strategic behavior to expand national power through commerce, a phenomenon stressed by Hirschman in his classic study. Although Japan tended to favor trading with the smaller countries, this tendency was not pronounced and it diminished significantly over time.

The previous studies mentioned above also showed that although Japan and the U.S. still retained their role as the two most important importers and exporters in the APEC region, their relative positions had slipped considerably between 1972 and 1992. Their respective shares of regional trade declined over time, while those of the Asian NIEs (especially China) had surged significantly.

Perhaps the most remarkable findings from the earlier studies were that the smaller APEC NIEs were generally able to increase their shares of the regional trade without becoming more dependent on their larger partners. That is, while expanding their national trade at a rate faster than the aggregate regional trade was growing, these countries -- such as South Korea, Thailand, and Indonesia -- also successfully diversified their trade relations, thus avoiding the fate of the Balkan countries in the 1930s. Contrary to the typical fears of the dependency theorists, the Asian NIEs' trade became less concentrated on a few partners. Indeed, by 1992 these countries had achieved a level of trade diversification comparable to and even more favorable than the U.S. and Japan.

Moreover, the composition of their trade portfolios underwent an important transformation during the past four decades or so. By the early 1990s, manufactured products had assumed an increasingly dominant share of the NIEs' exports as well as their imports. Concomitantly, the relative importance of foodstuffs and minerals in their trade declined significantly over time. The classic dependency characterization of unfavorable terms of trade -- due to the structural asymmetries involved in an exchange of unprocessed materials for manufactured goods -- hardly applies to countries such as South Korea, Singapore, Malaysia, and even Indonesia. Instead, these countries' trade now involves primarily exchanges of different kinds of manufactured products, such as textiles for computers and chemicals for automobiles. They have been rather successful in increasing the capital intensity and technological content of their production base, and thus have improved their relative position in the international division of labor. Compared to most Asian NIEs, agricultural and mineral products have in fact played a larger role in the exports of Canada, Australia, New Zealand and, indeed, the U.S. Thus, as far as the former countries are concerned, contemporary APEC trade patterns fail to support the premonitions of classic dependency or mercantilist formulations.

IV. Taiwan's Status

But what about Taiwan? Taiwan is of course an active participant in APEC trade. Using a gravity model of trade, Frankel[13] demonstrated empirically the existence of a regional system which included Taiwan. The United Nations (various years), however, does not report Taiwan's trade statistics, accounting for its omission in the analyses by Bobrow et al. and Chan.[14] Although unable to replicate exactly the same methodology of these earlier studies due to reasons of data comparability, this section will present some roughly comparable evidence for Taiwan based on the trade data reported by the Council for Economic Planning and Development.[15]

Three factors mitigate against the replication of the original methodology. First, the CEPD data fail to include all of the APEC trade partners included in the earlier studies. This source omitted two countries in the earlier sample: New Zealand and, more seriously, China.   Second, Hirschman's approach requires other countries' reports of the value of their exports to Taiwan in order to determine the value of Taiwan's imports from them (conversely, this approach uses other countries' reports of their imports from Taiwan in order to determine the island's exports to them). As already mentioned, standard U.N. sources do not include Taiwan in their data compilation. We will therefore settle for Taiwan's self-reports provided by the CEPD. Third, the trade data provided by the CEPD fail to distinguish between the C.I.F. and F.O.B. values of the goods traded, and their exact correspondence with the U.N. data is unclear.

With these caveats in mind, we proceed with the presentation and discussion of Taiwan's trade patterns during 1972-1992. These dates were chosen for reasons of comparability with the earlier studies, and eleven APEC members were included in the sample. They are Australia, Canada,

Hong Kong, Indonesia, Japan, South Korea, Malaysia, the Philippines, Singapore, Thailand, and the U.S. Besides New Zealand and China, the Latin American as well as several small APEC members were omitted from this analysis because of data unavailability.

We begin by asking the extent to which Taiwan contributed to the imports or exports of those APEC trade partners just identified. Of all the imports made by the latter countries from each other, what was the percentage accounted for by Taiwan's exports? Conversely, of all the exports sold by these countries to each other, what percentage was imported by Taiwan? The denominator in each case was the sum of imports or exports among the selected APEC members, excluding the country being studied (in this case, Taiwan). Hirschman called this measure WA for weighted average.

If a country is gaining importance in supplying others' import needs or, alternately, in buying others' export goods, its WA score should rise over time. Figure 5.1 offers some pertinent information showing Taiwan's relative importance in intra-APEC trade as indicated by the WA measure. It shows that while Taiwan's exports captured 3.52% of the other designated APEC members' regional imports in 1972, this figure rose to 7.48% in 1992. Likewise, Taiwan's imports as a share of the other countries' regional exports increased from 2.88% in 1972 to 6.47% in 1992. In both cases, Taiwan's portion of the expanding regional trade gained substantially. Its increased relative importance can be compared with the WA figures for the other APEC members reproduced from Bobrow et al. and Chan[16] and also reported in Table 5.1 (although, for reasons already mentioned, these figures are only roughly comparable).

Taiwan's evolving status in regional trade compares favorably not only with its own prior position (as indicated by the difference in its trade share between 1972 and 1992), but also with the changing positions of other Asian NIEs such as South Korea and Thailand. Among those countries included in Table 5.1, only China demonstrated significantly greater relative gains in regional trade. While the Asian NIEs collectively improved their relative importance in regional trade, the more mature economies did less well. Some such as Japan more or less held on to their earlier position, whereas others such as the U.S. and especially Canada experienced a rather sharp decline in their position. The overall impression conveyed by the information in Table 5.1 therefore points to the commercial ascendance of the Asian NIEs at the expense of the latter countries. The NIEs have over time become collectively more important customers for each others' traded products. There is little in Table 5.1 that would support the fate assigned by the classic dependency and mercantilist theorists to the smaller and more trade-dependent countries.

Table 5.1 Aggregate Importance in APEC Trade: The WA Index

	Imports (by other countries)		Exports (by other countries)	
	1972	1992	1972	1992
Taiwan	3.5	7.5	2.9	6.50
Australia	3.3	2.9	5.3	3.44
Canada	26.2	13.3	31.0	14.80
China	1.5	8.1	2.3	12.70
Hong Kong	3.8	9.8	2.8	5.00
Indonesia	1.9	1.3	2.7	3.20
Japan	20.4	18.2	28.5	29.20
Korea, South	2.8	5.5	2.0	5.80
Malaysia	1.7	3.0	2.2	4.00
New Zealand	1.1	0.7	1.2	0.80
Philippines	1.5	1.2	1.6	1.00
Singapore	3.1	5.6	1.4	4.30
Thailand	1.4	2.8	1.1	2.60
United States	57.8	43.0	56.4	36.20

A significant insight of the dependency school is that the smaller and more trade-dependent countries are vulnerable to economic coercion because their trade tends to be limited to a few large partners. In discussing Nazi Germany's trade offensive, Hirschman documented Berlin's deliberate attempt to divert trade to the smaller trading countries. A given amount of imports or exports would account for a low percentage of the overall foreign commerce of a large trading power, but a high percentage of that of a small trading country. Thus, a country embarked on a policy of strategic trade would steer its imports and exports toward the smaller trading countries in order to seek trade-based influence over them. This was the logic of Hirschman's analysis, and the focus of several subsequent studies.[17]

Accordingly, Hirschman's study also developed a UA index (for unweighted average) which was intended to measure a country's average -- in contrast to WA's focus on its aggregate -- importance across each of its trade partners. Whereas WA measures Country X's share of the sum of trade among A, B, C and so on, UA measures the average of its trade shares with each of the latter. Table 5.2 presents the UA scores for the selected APEC members (again keeping in mind the proviso that the basis for Taiwan's figures is not identical to those for the other APEC countries).

Table 5.2 Aggregate Importance in APEC Trade: The VA Index

	Imports (by other countries)		Exports (by other countries)	
	1972	1992	1972	1992
Taiwan	3.6	7.2	3.1	5.2
Australia	4.4	4.6	9.0	6.3
Canada	7.7	5.6	9.3	5.0
China	1.1	10.5	4.2	9.9
Hong Kong	7.8	8.6	2.4	5.2
Indonesia	2.8	1.6	2.4	3.1
Japan	27.8	20.9	37.0	30.9
Korea, South	1.7	4.8	1.1	5.8
Malaysia	6.2	3.9	3.6	4.7
New Zealand	1.4	1.1	1.4	1.2
Philippines	1.5	1.3	0.8	0.7
Singapore	6.5	7.5	2.9	6.5
Thailand	1.6	3.0	1.8	2.3
United States	37.5	36.3	31.8	0.8

Naturally, a country's UA readings need not correspond to its WA readings. During the 1930s, German commercial power derived not only from the fact that its foreign trade was expanding faster than that of Britain and France, but also because Berlin's trade was on the average more important to its partners in comparison with London and Paris. A comparison of the figures in Tables 5.1 and 5.2 show that in both imports and exports, Japan's average importance to its APEC partners was greater than its aggregate importance. This tendency, however, diminished over time, so that the UA and WA figures were less discrepant in 1992 than in 1972. In contrast to Japan, the figures indicate that the U.S. had a greater aggregate importance than average importance in APEC trade. For Taiwan, the UA and WA figures were quite similar.

A more systematic way of studying any discrepancies between the UA and WA scores is to divide the former by the latter. The result is Hirschman's R index, which was used to identify those countries showing a distinct bias in favor of trading with the smaller countries. The R index thus provides *prima facie* evidence of strategic trade intended to foster asymmetric dependency on the part of the latter countries. Table 5.3 offers some pertinent evidence, again juxtaposing Taiwan's scores with those of the other APEC countries reported earlier by Bobrow et al. and Chan.[18]

A low R reading indicates a bias in favor of trading with the larger countries, whereas a high R reading indicates a bias in favor of trading with the smaller countries (again, large and small in this context refer to trade volume and not physical size). The figures for Taiwan show that its trade has been historically rather evenly balanced between the larger and smaller APEC partners, with the R scores in 1972 falling very close to the neutral reading 100. It continued this neutrality in contributing to the others' imports in 1992, although by this year its purchase of others' exports had become more oriented toward the larger countries. The latter tendency, however, was not especially acute. Regarding their imports, China and the Philippines also exhibited this tendency and to a stronger extent. Given its close trade ties with the U.S., Canada had an especially pronounced tendency of favoring trade with the larger countries.

If a persistent pattern of favoring trade with the smaller countries is indicative of strategic behavior, this characterization did not apply to the U.S. whose trade showed the opposite tendency of concentrating on the larger countries. Japan did show a tendency to trade more with the smaller countries in the early 1970s, but this bias had almost disappeared by the 1990s. As for China, its trade in 1992 displayed contrasting patterns. While China's exports favored the smaller trading economies, its imports favored the larger ones. Countries that demonstrated the strongest bias toward trading with their smaller partners were not the U.S., Japan, or China; they were Malaysia, Singapore, and New Zealand.

As already noted, partner concentration has been an abiding concern of *dependentistas* and mercantilists due its vulnerability implications for foreign coercion. Table 5.4 presents a final set of figures based on

Table 5.3 Bias Towards the Smaller APEC Trade Partners: The R Index Imports

	Imports (by other countries)		Exports (by other countries)	
	1972	1992	1972	1992
Taiwan	102.8	96.3	107.6	80.7
Australia	133.4	155.9	171.1	186.8
Canada	29.4	42.5	30.1	34.0
China	68.8	129.2	182.4	77.3
Hong Kong	207.1	88.3	87.2	102.8
Indonesia	148.2	126.3	90.4	96.3
Japan	136.2	114.8	129.7	106.0
Korea, South	61.0	88.2	56.3	100.5
Malaysia	360.9	131.4	165.2	116.6
New Zealand	130.3	152.8	119.4	154.4
Philippines	102.7	107.3	52.5	65.8
Singapore	208.8	133.8	215.9	149.6
Thailand	114.2	104.2	171.6	91.5
United States	64.2	84.4	56.3	85.3

Hirschman's formulation. Details about computing the index of partner concentration were provided in Bobrow et al.[19] Suffice it to say that this index varies from 100 (indicating exclusive trade with only one partner) to 30.15 (when trade is divided equally among eleven partners). The figures for Taiwan are closer to the low end of the spectrum, thus suggesting a substantial diversification of its trade partners. Indeed, comparing the 1972 figures with the 1992 ones, it is evident that both Taiwan's imports and exports became over time less concentrated on a few partners. This evidence should dampen concerns about the political vulnerability that can stem from an over-reliance on one or two partners.

Below the figures for Taiwan, Table 5.4 also reports the degree of partner concentration for the other selected APEC members. The lower bound of the concentration index for these countries, however, is 28.87; this is the score when a country distributes its trade equally among twelve partners. As can be seen from the figures for the other Asian NIEs, they were

Table 5.4 Partner Concentration in APEC Trade

	Imports (by other countries)		Exports (by other countries)	
	1972	1992	1972	1992
Taiwan	60.8	53.7	55.6	49.6
Australia	52.2	46.8	65.5	46.2
Canada	88.9	86.7	90.0	87.9
China	63.7	59.3	56.1	54.5
Hong Kong	49.0	53.0	69.7	58.4
Indonesia	54.1	43.9	69.5	50.7
Japan	50.3	43.8	57.9	49.4
Korea, South	63.8	50.9	63.7	46.1
Malaysia	47.3	47.8	50.4	45.7
New Zealand	53.1	48.7	49.6	42.5
Philippines	57.1	43.8	65.7	58.7
Singapore	43.4	40.7	40.6	41.8
Thailand	60.4	47.8	43.3	46.7
United States	61.1	49.4	63.4	47.5

like Taiwan able to avoid excessive concentration of their trade with a few partners. Moreover, they were also able to increase their diversification of trade partners over time. Indeed, in 1992 the degree of their trade concentration was generally comparable to that of Japan and the U.S. Among the APEC countries studied in this paper, Canada had clearly the highest degree of partner concentration. Its trade was overwhelmingly oriented toward the U.S.

Conclusion

This paper began with a concern for the political consequences of trade. Trade, it is argued, can be a double-edged sword that enhances mutual responsiveness as well as supply vulnerability. Although we did not study the alleged positive influence of trade on international peace and stability, we did present some evidence showing that it at least did not in the case of APEC generally and Taiwan particularly produce those structural properties that pose a threat to national autonomy. This conclusion, however, needs to be tempered somewhat because this analysis has not included Taiwan's trade with Mainland China due to the lack of systematic data. Nevertheless, the evidence on Taiwan's APEC trade developed in this study confirms broader patterns uncovered in earlier analyses. These patterns point to impressive status improvement on the part of Asia's NIEs, which were able to successfully increase their relative shares of regional trade while at the same time reducing their dependency on the U.S. and Japan. A rising trade tide has lifted all boats, but especially the smaller ones representing the NIEs. Moreover, the NIEs' trade became substantially more diversified between 1972 and 1992, so that they became more important partners for each other. At least up to the early 1990s, the trend has been in the direction of greater trade interdependence rather than dependence. Although it would be premature to declare the dawning of a security community among the APEC members, some of the worst premonitions of the mercantilist and dependency writers have not come to pass.

Notes

1.   Karl W. Deutsch, Sidney A. Burrell, Robert A. Kann, Maurice Lee, Jr., Martin Lichtenman, Raymond E. Lindgren, Francis L. Loewenheim, and Richard W. Van Wagenen. 1957. *Political Community and the North Atlantic Area: International Organization in the Light of Historical Experience*. New York: Greenwood.
2.   Immanuel Kant. 1957 [1795]. *Perpetual Peace*, translated by Lewis White Beck. New York: Bobbs-Merrill.
3.   Robert O. Keohane and Joseph Nye. 1977. *Power and Interdependence: World Politics in Transition*. Boston: Little, Brown.
4.   Robert Putnam. 1988. "Diplomacy and Domestic Politics: The Logic of Two-Level Games." *International Organization* 42: 427-460.
5.   John R. Oneal and Bruce M. Russett. 1997. "The Classical Liberals Were Right: Democracy, Interdependence, and Conflict: 1950-1985." *International Studies*

              Quarterly 41: 267-293. John R. Oneal, Frances H. Oneal, Zeev Maoz, and Bruce M. Russett. 1996. "The Liberal Peace: Interdependence, Democracy, and International Conflict, 1950-85." *Journal of Peace Research* 33: 11-28.

6.   Albert O. Hirschman. 1980 [1945]. *National Power and the Structure of Foreign Trade.* Berkeley: University of California Press.

7.   Samir Amin. 1974. *Accumulation on a World Scale: A Critique of the Theory of Underdevelopment.* New York: Monthly Review Press. Celso Furtado. 1970. *Economic Development of Latin America: A Survey from Colonial Times to the Cuban Revolution.* Cambridge: Cambridge University Press.

8.   Friedrich List. 1956 [1841]. *The National System of Political Economy.* Philadelphia Lippincott.

9.   Davis B. Bobrow, Steve Chan, and Simon Reich. 1996. "Southeast Asian Prospects and Realities: American Hopes and Fears." *Pacific Review* 9: 1-30.

10.   Albert O. Hirschman. 1980 [1945].

11.   Alice H. Amsden. 1989. *Asia's Next Giant: South Korea and Late Industrialization.* New York: Columbia University Press. Wade. 1990. David Yoffie. 1983. *Power and Protectionism: Strategies of the Newly Industrializing Countries.* New York: Columbia University Press.

12.   Davis B. Bobrow, Steve Chan, and Simon Reich. 1998. "Trade, Power and APEC: Hirschman Revisited." *International Interactions*: forthcoming. Steve Chan. 1997. "APEC's Evolving Trade Structure." Paper presented at the conference on "Europe, North America, and Asia Pacific: Cooperation or Conflict?" University of Calgary, October 24-25, Calgary, Alberta.

13.   Jeffrey A. Frankel. 1993. "Is Japan Creating a Yen Bloc in East Asia and the Pacific?"   Pp. 53-85 in Jeffrey A. Frankel and Miles Kahler (eds.), *Regionalism and Rivalry: Japan and the United States in Pacific Asia.* Chicago: University of Chicago Press.

14.   Davis B. Bobrow, et al. "Trade, Power and APEC: Hirschman Revisited." Steve Chan. "APEC's Evolving Trade Structure."

15.   Council for Economic Planning and Development. 1997. *Taiwan Statistical Data Book: 1997.* Taipei: Author.

16.   Davis B. Bobrow, et al. "Trade, Power and APEC: Hirschman Revisited." Steve Chan. "APEC's Evolving Trade Structure."

17.   Davis B. Bobrow, et al. 1998. Paul Marer. 1974. "The Political Economy of Soviet Relations with Eastern Europe." Pp. 231-260 in Steven J. Rosen and James R. Kurth (eds.), *Testing Theories of Economic Imperialism.* Lexington, MA: Lexington Books.   Michael Michaely. 1962. *Concentration in International Trade.* Amsterdam: North-Holland Publishing Company.   R. Harrison Wagner. 1988. "Economic Interdependence, Bargaining Power, and   Political Influence." *International Organization* 42: 461-483.

18.   Davis B. Bobrow, et al. "Trade, Power and APEC: Hirschman Revisited." Steve Chan. "APEC's Evolving Trade Structure."

19.   Davis B. Bobrow, et al. "Trade, Power and APEC: Hirschman Revisited."

6 Risk Diversification: Ensuring Taiwan's Security

ALEXANDER C. TAN with SCOTT WALKER and TSUNG-CHI YU

Introduction

With the election of the Democratic Progressive Party's presidential candidate -- Chen Shui-bian -- in March 2000 the question of how to best insure Taiwan's security again became a focal point.   Will the new administration take Taiwan into a collision course with its adversary -- PRC? Or will we see a gradual evolution and more peaceful resolution or understanding of the cross-Straits relations in the future?   These are questions that will preoccupy policy makers in Taipei, Beijing, and Washington.   Unfortunately, there are no clear cut answers to these questions.   In this chapter, we suggest one way to understand Taiwan's national security policy is by examining the evolution from the so-called high politics of international relations to low politics.   The saying that "politics stop at the water's edge" may be precise in describing Taiwan's national security policy during the Cold War. This, however, is not appropriate to describe Taiwan's national security policy post-1979 and post-Cold War. The changing security environment in the Asia-Pacific region coupled with the historic transformation in Taiwan's domestic political environment, i.e., political liberalization and democratization require us to carefully examine the role of the democratization and the search for national identity in understanding Taiwan's security policy (the so-called "low politics").

In the next section, we briefly trace the "high politics" of Taiwan's security policy with particular emphasis on the use of development and trade as a security mechanism. In the second section, we discuss the peaceful transformation of Taiwan from an authoritarian developmental state into a democratic polity. In this discussion, we examine the implications of Taiwan's democratization and pluralization of politics and policymaking and their implication to Taiwan's national security. In the third section, we briefly examine the role of the United States in cross-Strait relations and the changes in cross-Strait interactions. We conclude by briefly discussing the implications of the converging goals of politicians on both sides of the Taiwan Straits that is complicated by the diverging conduct of politics in the two polities.

Economic Statecraft and Taiwan's Security

Taiwan's search for its security began in earnest when the Kuomintang (KMT) lost its civil war with the Chinese Communists. Since 1949, Taiwan has been under some kind of threat of an invasion from the People's Republic of China (PRC), both physically and verbally. Nonetheless, with the United States acting as Taiwan's security guarantor from 1949-1979, PRC is kept at arms length and thereby providing Taiwan some breathing space.

With the rapprochement between the United States and China following U.S. President Richard Nixon's visit to Beijing and the eventual de-recognition of Taiwan by the United States in 1979 by President Jimmy Carter, the nature of Taiwan's security blanket transformed dramatically. Instead of relative clarity, Taiwan has to deal with the so-called strategic ambiguity. Of course, Taiwan felt that it was left to fend for itself immediately following 1979.

Being diplomatically isolated, Taiwan needed to carve out an "independent" national security policy. Most foci on national security have always been on military issues, and less attention has been placed on the use of trade as part of statecraft. Indeed, while Taiwan's rapid economic growth and industrialization are an oft-studied topic in economic development, we understand much less about how Taiwan has used it as a tool to gain security. As Karl Deutsch (1957) suggests, international trade can stimulate acceptance and mutual responsiveness among trading nations.[1] As Steve Chan writes, "increasing commercial and noncommercial contact has the effect of deepening and widening networks of cross-national interests and institutions. These networks and shared norms underpin the rise of a 'security community'."[2]

Taiwan's active participation in the world's trading regime, particularly after the United States switched its recognition to the PRC, can be seen in the light of its need to secure its own survival by being firmly attached to the global economy and the production process. As Keohane defines it, regimes are "sets of implicit of explicit principles, norms, rules, and decision-making procedures around which actor expectations converge."[3] Keohane suggests that:

> within the context of a regime, help can be extended by those in a position to do so, on the assumption that such regime-supporting behavior will be reciprocated in the future. States may demand that others follow the norm of generalized commitment even if they are thereby required to supply it themselves, because the result will facilitate agreements that in the long run can be expected to be beneficial for all concerned.[4]

Seen in this light, Taiwan's motivation for trade is related to some version of the neo-realist and neo-liberal views of ensuring security through trade and functional relationships.[5]

Indeed, one way to understand Taiwan's national security is by economic statecraft. In fact, the growth of the Taiwanese economy (in general) and the acceleration of growth in Taiwan's international trade (in particular) become an important tool to firmly integrate Taiwan into the international economy. By firmly integrating Taiwan's economy with the international economy, Taiwan makes itself an important player in the world manufacturing economy. As a result, this transformation to a capital and knowledge intensive industrial structure in some ways decreases the substitutability of Taiwan in the world economy and increases the vulnerability of Taiwan's important trading partners. By binding Taiwan's economic "fate" to the world, Taiwan can avail itself of some security as the world becomes vulnerable to instability in Taiwan.

In spite of Taiwan's diplomatic isolation, its total trade volume has grown over the years making Taiwan one of the world's top trading nations. Table 6.1 shows Taiwan's trade with its neighboring countries and the United States. Trade with the United States has always been an important component of the Taiwan economy. In fact, Table 6.1 shows that the severing of official diplomatic relations in 1979 between the United States and Taiwan has not affected the growth of two-way trade. Trade with Japan has also grown in total volume from U.S. $6.81 billion in 1979 to $41.2 billion in 1996.

The maintenance of strong trade relations between Taiwan, Japan, and the United States has contributed to expanded commercial and noncommercial contacts between Taiwan and its two largest trading partners. Taiwan's contact with Japan and the United States goes beyond traditional government to government format but extends to business and civic contacts as well.   For example, Taiwan has been actively engaged in non-governmental organizations such as the Pacific Economic Cooperation Conference and the Pacific Basin Economic Council. These organizations though non-governmental have strong governmental participation. Furthermore, strong trading relations with Japan, the United States, and the European Union make a strong case that Taiwan should be part of the World Trade Organization.[6]

Table 6.1 Taiwan's Trade Volume with U.S.A. and Neighbors
(In millions)

Country	1979	1985	1990	1996
USA	9.03	19.5	34.4	46.8
Japan	6.81	9.01	24.3	41.2
Singapore	0.54	1.16	3.61	7.36
Thailand	0.25	0.38	1.87	4.46
Malaysia	0.46	0.67	2.11	6.52
Philippines	0.27	0.34	1.05	2.77
Hong Kong	1.34	2.86	10.0	28.5

Source: Taiwan Statistical Data Book, 1997.

Through the benefits of trade expansion and the extension of Taiwan's business contacts in Japan and the United States, Taiwan has created an informal security community that may work to her benefit. As a case in point, in the renegotiation of the Japan-United States security framework, Japan did not reject the idea that its naval vessels will provide necessary support for U.S. naval operations in case of conflict in the area.[7] Based on the PRC's reaction, this is an implicit agreement that should the United States get involved in a cross-Taiwan Strait conflict, Japan can probably play an important support role.

Though the revised United States -- Japan security guidelines do not explicitly include Taiwan in the security scope, American and Japanese officials have not explicitly ruled it out either. American officials emphasize that the new defense agreement is not aimed at any individual nation (in vague reference to China) but it would not completely rule out that Taiwan is covered by the revised United States -- Japan security guidelines.[8] Interestingly, despite strategically ambiguous language by both Japanese and American officials, one ranking Japanese official was quoted as stating that the revised security guidelines between Japan and the United States do cover a military conflict in the Taiwan Strait because of concerns about possible Chinese military action against the island of Taiwan.[9] Similarly, in discussion of a Theater Missile Defense (TMD) system that is designed to provide missile defense to Asian allies of the United States (like Japan), the United States have approached Taiwan in contributing to efforts at developing this missile defense system. Much to the consternation of the People's Republic of China, Taiwan's likely participation may also mean that it will be within the protected area of the Theater Missile Defense system.

Trade plays an important role in Taiwan's strategy to ensure its own security and survival as a sovereign nation-state. Since the 1990s, however, Taiwan was also able to play an important role as important financier in the region. Taiwan's large capital surplus and its huge foreign exchange reserves are seen within Taiwan's government not only in commercial terms but also as an important tool in the fight against diplomatic isolation.

In November of 1993, Taiwan announced at the first Asia-Pacific Economic Cooperation meeting in Seattle that it had decided to embark on the "Go South" policy, a program of investment and trade designed to increase Taiwanese investment in Southeast Asia -- a region with a high level of strategic and economic importance to Taiwan. Otherwise called "Operation Outline for Strengthening Economic and Trading Relations with Southeast Asia," the Go South policy was aimed at six Southeast Asian countries: Indonesia, Singapore, Thailand, the Philippines, Malaysia, and Vietnam.

The basic idea of this policy is that Taiwan would be seen as a major supplier of capital and technology into the region. The strategy of the Go South policy was to provide the industrial and agricultural know-how, as well as the capital required (in the form of loans, investment banking arrangements), etc., to make Taiwan an important economic partner in the economies of the region. Of course, an important benefit of successful implementation of this policy would be that these countries would be more likely to value Taiwanese friendship. Clearly, then, underlying the economic purposes of Go South was an attempt by Taiwan to bolster its political stability in the region by strengthening economic relationships with its Southeast Asian neighbors.

This relationship, of course, was not looked upon favorably by the Chinese government. First, China resented the economic competition in the region, although a Taiwanese presence was already strong in Southeast Asia, particularly in Malaysia and Thailand.

The Go South campaign was an outgrowth of a well-played visit President Lee made to Southeast Asia in 1994, which opened the region to Taiwanese investors. The campaign encouraged companies to find cheap labor and manufacturing costs in the region, a move that effectively warmed political relations between the island and Southeast Asian nations. On that trip, bitterly opposed by China, Lee met with top officials from the Philippines, Indonesia, and Thailand, promising to help the region develop agricultural and oil resources.

There were four stated goals of the Go South Policy:

1) Expand two-way economic, trade, and investment relations with Southeast Asia;

2) Assist Taiwan's enterprises in finding beneficial production and distribution bases in Southeast Asia, expanding their management size, and reducing the degree of trade dependence on mainland China;

3) Help Southeast Asian nations -- based on the principle of mutual benefit -- create job opportunities, raise people's annual incomes, and encourage economic prosperity, thus strengthening Taiwan's substantive relations with the nations of Southeast Asia;

4) Participate in the activities of international economic organizations in Southeast Asia.

Since 1994, under the Go South policy, Taiwan has encouraged investment in Southeast Asia. According to statistics provided by Southeast Asian countries, the cumulative total of investment by Taiwanese businesses in Southeast Asia reached U.S. $40 billion in 1999. In that year, the amount of bilateral trade between Taiwan and Southeast Asia was U.S. $26.59 billion.

Table 6.2 shows Taiwan's outward direct investment since the 1990s. As evident in Taiwan's outward investments, the United States is a large recipient of Taiwanese investments. In the 1990s, however, Taiwan's investments in Southeast Asia have taken a large proportion of all Taiwanese outward investments. Part of the stimulus for the increase in Southeast Asian investments is the industrial restructuring occurring within Taiwan itself. As labor costs and the Taiwanese dollar has appreciated in the 1990s, Taiwanese labor-intensive industries have moved to Southeast Asia to remain competitive. These outward movement of Taiwanese capital to Southeast Asia has made Taiwan one of the top three largest investors in the region.

Table 6.2 Taiwan's Outward Direct Investments
  (In percentage share of total outward direct investments)

	'90	'91	'92	'93	'94	'95	'96	'97
USA	28	16	17	11	6	10	8	12
SE Asia	37	39	27	9	15	13	17	14
China	n/a	10	22	66	37	45	36	36

Source: Investment Evaluation Commission, Ministry of Economic Affairs.

Interestingly, as shown in both Tables 6.1 and 6.2, Taiwan's trade and investment to either Hong Kong and China are also a large percentage of Taiwan's total trade and outward investments. By 1996, Hong Kong has become the third largest trading partner of Taiwan and the PRC is recipient of more than one-third of all Taiwanese outward investments. Increase trade and investment with the PRC may be a cause for concern to Taiwan as it gets increasingly absorbed into the PRC's economic sphere. However, this concern neglects the fact that as the PRC and Taiwan increases bilateral trade and investments, the expansion of common interests and institutions may serve to dissuade both sides to disrupt this mutually beneficial relationship. As in a simultaneous iterative game between two players, players see a benefit to maintaining the status quo which yields greater benefits for both sides.

Democratization and the Search for National Identity

In the last fourteen years, Taiwan's political economy has undergone tremendous transformation from a developmental authoritarian state to a democracy. While certain characteristic of Taiwan's democracy shows its uniqueness when compared with the advanced industrial democracies, one thing that is comparable to Western democracies is the increasing influence of public opinion on decision-making from the introduction of competitive elections. For Taiwan's political elites, the end of the post-Cold War period requires some tinkering of Taiwan's national security strategy. Catching the bandwagon of democratization in the third wave became a likely strategy.

It is important to note, though, that the realization that democratization can be a strategy for national security was not directly borne out of careful planning and design by the ruling KMT elites but a consequence of conflicts and struggles within the domestic political arena between the majority islanders and the minority mainlanders. These conflicts have underscored Taiwanese politics since the forced exile of the KMT to the island of Taiwan. With rapid economic growth and the eventual creation of a large middle class, the KMT was forced to open the political system through the process of "Taiwanization" of the party and the government.[10] Because of Taiwanization, the mainlanders grip on power slowly eroded and political democratization settled in.[11]

For Taiwan and the Kuomintang, the introduction of democracy in the island increases its political legitimacy in the international arena. Efforts at political liberalization began under the late President Chiang Ching-Kuo when in 1986 the government allowed the formation of the first opposition party in Taiwan -- the Democratic Progressive Party (DPP). Though the opposition in Taiwan has always existed during the Kuomintang (KMT) rule under the umbrella name of *"Tangwai"* which means literally "outside of the KMT," the formation of the DPP is significant because it marks the true beginning of organized competitive politics in Taiwan. The formation of the DPP is also significant in that it signals a shift within the KMT of allowing political liberalization to occur.

Political liberalization and eventually democracy was not fully initiated until the death of President Chiang Ching-Kuo and the succession of President Lee Teng-hui. President Lee, being the first islander that held this top office, pushed for greater indigenization of the ruling party, the military, and the government. Democratization in Taiwan became an extension and probably unintended consequence of Taiwanization. As Cal Clark aptly states,

> democratization in Taiwan appears to have been delayed considerably in terms of its relatively advanced level of social and economic modernization in the mid-1980s, it certainly conformed to two central postulates of the modernization model 1) than an educated middle-class will exert considerable pressure for reform on an authoritarian regime and 2) that political liberalization will result in the party

system's providing better interest representation on the major issues facing a society.[12]

This has resulted in a political system characterized by the emergence of cleavages suppressed during the authoritarian period and the increased complexity in domestic politics.

In spite of its origins in Taiwan, democracy is a way of clearly distinguishing Taiwan from the authoritarianism of the PRC.[13] In the eyes of its neighboring countries and the West, Taiwan's democratization presents a clear signal that it is part of a "democratic alliance." From a Kantian perspective, the respect for the rule of law both domestically and internationally allows Taiwan to be part of that security community of like-minded nations. Research has shown that countries that are democratic do not generally go to war with each other.[14] For Taiwan then, the strategic implication of its democratization is that by taking the moral high ground, Taiwan can secure for it a place among the "democratic alliance." Democratization can be a double-edged sword, though. The introduction of competitive elections has made Taiwan develop a party system that largely reflects the ethnic cleavage that is most salient in Taiwan's domestic politics. This ethnic cleavage is reflected in the debate about the national identity issue. The democratic and plural political environment allows for an internal debate on the prickly issue of reunification or independence. As a result, "the developmental states (as in Taiwan) have become less dominant in their relations with social groups -- an outcome caused by the success of their economic strategy."[15]

That accountability to the whims and desires of the electorate becomes inevitable in democratic politics. This in turn leads to a tendency toward the maintenance of the status quo, since the status quo (that is neither formal independence nor reunification) is a position that prevents open conflict with PRC. As Cal Clark states,

> Clearly, the ROC's citizens (particularly the middle class who has the most to lose) fear that a premature commitment to either Independence or Reunification could destroy the social, economic, and political progress that Taiwan has already made. In addition, except for relatively small minorities, the island's citizens do not evidently see the future as a stark choice between these two alternatives...a public opinion poll...reported ...that both Reunification or Independence were acceptable by approximately two-to-one margins if the change in status could be achieved without the dangers now associated with it (subordination to a communist dictatorship for Reunification and Chinese retaliation for Independence). Thus,

neither party can be seen as threatening the status quo too greatly -- which keeps both levels of the "game" acceptable to most constituencies in Taiwan, as well as to the Chinese authorities.[16]

The adoption of the status quo as an equilibrium strategy allows Taiwan to buy time to allow peaceful democratic transformation in the PRC to achieve the so-called "democratic peace." Having said this, the maintenance of the status quo also means active engagement with the PRC in the economic front.

As evidenced by President Chen Shui-bian proclamation to open direct links to the three islets of Kinmen (Quemoy), Matsu, and Penghu (the Pescadores) to the PRC represent a fundamental policy shift in cross-Strait relations in favor of regional economic integration based on mutual interests. We argue that such a benign gesture will further mitigate mutual conflicts and stabilize security uncertainties presented by peaceful transition of the reigns of government in Taiwan. The combination of Taiwan's comparative advantage in banking, communication, high technology, and market expertise combined with the abundant supply of labor and land in China present a win-win scenario (a positive sum game) for both sides to build on in the future.

We expect that with greater democratization of Taiwan, world opinion of Taiwan also becomes increasingly more favorable. As a case in point, positive coverage of Taiwan in media in the United States has been increasing since Taiwan's political liberalization. This positive coverage of Taiwan peaked in 1995 and 1996 as Taiwan prepares for its first popular election of the president. Indeed, in the months leading up to the presidential election in March 1996, the PRC conducted missile exercises off the Taiwan coasts and continually warned the island of "grave consequences" if an independence-supporter is elected. Resulting from these military threats, world coverage of Taiwan has increased. Interestingly, the coverage about Taiwan is positive and seems to imply that Taiwan is an important part of the world economy.

The Role of the United States in Cross-Strait Relations

In any discussion of Taiwan-PRC relations, examining the role of the United States is imperative. Before the de-recognition of Taiwan by the United States in 1979, the United States has played the key role in explicitly securing Taiwan's security. After the break in official diplomatic relations, the United States' commitment is largely spelled out for in the Taiwan Relations Act of 1979. Nonetheless, the commitment to a one-China policy by the United States government on the one hand and living up to the spirit of the Taiwan Relations Act has placed the United States in a difficult spot defining its own position in cross-Strait relations. This so-called strategic ambiguity in American policy toward Taiwan and the PRC has been deemed important in maintaining relative peace and the status quo but it has also contributed to substantial change in the American approach toward its relationship with Taiwan and the PRC.

This change is characterized by the neo-realist approach emphasizing trade, investment and the importance of international organization is dealing with the PRC and Taiwan.[17] The use of trade and investment to replace old military confrontation may be the preferred strategy of the United States. The Clinton Administration's "Three-No" policy that includes a) no independent Taiwan; b) no two Chinas or one Taiwan, one China; and c) no Taiwan membership in intergovernmental organizations served to define the United States position in cross-Strait relations.[18] Simultaneously, Clinton's clarification of the "Three-No" policy acts as a catalyst for Taiwan and the PRC to re-calibrate their approach to bilateral relations by emphasizing the maintenance of the status quo.[19]

For Taiwan, the United States' "Three-No" policy constrains the possible options for its own dealings with the PRC. Instead of focusing solely on sovereignty issues, the "Three-No" policy forces the two sides to move to other areas of mutual agreements such as economic cooperation and establishment of possible direct links on shipping, communication, and transportation.[20] Furthermore, the relative clarity of American position against a unilateral declaration of Taiwan independence has forced Taiwan's leadership to tone down its own rhetoric and action toward an independent Taiwan so as not to anger the PRC and the United States.[21] More recently, President Chen's action of toning down Taiwan's summer war games and military exercises signals the island's commitment to avoid inflaming relations with the PRC. This move to placate Beijing is also coupled by statements that Taiwan is ready to defend itself if attacked signals the new administration's commitment to maintaining the status quo.[22]

In the case of China-U.S. interactions, the opening of American markets to PRC exports and the increase investments by American businesses in the PRC has expanded the basis of common interests between the United States and China. These common interests resulting from functional relations (e.g., trade and investments) can spill over to other areas such as common security.

The approval by the United States Congress of China's permanent trade benefits on 19 September 2000 supports our arguments that American policymakers hope that by bringing China into the international trading regime it may drastically change China's cost calculation in resolving conflicts by use of force.   According to neo-realist thinking, as functional and economic interactions increase in frequency and iteration, a state's incentive to be non-confrontational and cooperative in its international dealings increases. That is, as the PRC economy continues to benefit from participation in the international trading regime, the benefits of trade and maintaining the regime outweighs any benefit associated with destroying established equilibrium. As Gill and Reilly insightfully point out,

> Since the People's Republic initially opened up in the 1970s, China's strict sovereign prerogatives have been gradually eroded. Today the nexus where defense of Chinese sovereignty meets the imperative of engaging the outside world defines both the limits and the possibilities of enmeshing China within international society. The challenge for the international community is to understand the dynamics of China's sovereignty-integration nexus and to identify policies that will strengthen Beijing's commitment to international peace and stability.[23]

This is the challenge that exists for the United States and Taiwan in its dealings with the People's Republic of China.

Conclusion

To obtain the optimum balance between the goals of growth, order, and security, East Asian political leaders may find that it may lead each country to diverging conduct and paths. Chan suggests that "economic prosperity may increase the danger of war because it makes armament expenditures more affordable and influences leaders to be more aggressive and self-confident in their foreign policies."[24]   If this is correct, then, "the recent economic dynamism and expansion of capitalist East Asian countries may suggest a greater danger of warfare and military competition in the years ahead."[25] This would suggest that while the goals of leaders in both sides of the Taiwan Strait may be converging, the paths to achieving those goals are diverging.

Having said this though, we would be remiss not to consider the role of the United States in cross-Strait relations.   As the hegemon, it is in the interest of the United States to maintain the status quo and prevent an open conflict between the PRC and Taiwan.[26] To maintain relative peace in the area then, American policymakers want to actively engage the PRC and draw the PRC into the rubric of existing international regime ala the functionalist argument. This will not only require the PRC to comply with economic norms such as the protection of the intellectual property rights, but also with political norms such as to abide by the international human rights and the principle of "negotiation instead of confrontation." The U.S. policy thinking is based on the premise that the higher the trade interdependence between the PRC and the USA or the PRC and Taiwan, the less likely the PRC will invade Taiwan by force.

Notes

1.   Karl Deutsch, *Political Community and the North Atlantic Area* (New York: Greenwood).
2.   Steve Chan, "Taiwan in APEC's Trade Structure," in this book.
3.   Robert Keohane, "The Demand for International Regimes," *International Organization*, Vol. 36, No. 2, p. 141.
4.   Ibid, p. 159.
5.   We are suggesting that Taiwan's approach can be seen as both a neo-realist and neo-liberal prescription. As a neo-realist prescription concern for balance of power and power dynamics are considered together with the importance of trade and economics in achieving security. As a neo-liberal prescription, Taiwan is also concerned with developing a complex network of interdependence to maintain peace and create a security community to ensure its national security.
6.   Taiwan's application to be a part of the World Trade Organization is currently held up by the status of the People's Republic of China (PRC). With the passing of the Permanent Normal Trading Relation with China in the United States Congress, the PRC's application is considered to be accepted. As a consequence of this, Taiwan's application will be successfully resolved as well. Interestingly, the issue here is not whether Taiwan should be a part of the WTO but how should it be admitted. Fortunately for Taiwan, the issue of Taiwan's national identity in world governmental bodies have long been settled with what is called the Olympic model. That is, Taiwan will be. admitted as full members of international organizations under a name (Chinese Taipei, in the Olympic case) that will acknowledge that it is a part of China but it currently has jurisdiction over the island.   This model, however, does not acknowledge China's claim on Taiwan nor Taiwan's claim on China.
7.   Dennis Hickey, "The Revise U.S.-Japan Security Guidelines: Implications for

132   *Taiwan's National Security: Dilemmas and Opportunities*

Beijing and Taipei," paper presented at the Conference on Dilemmas and Opportunities: Taiwan's National Security, Dallas, Texas, April 1998.

8. Ibid, p. 9.
9. Ibid, p.10; Nicholas Kristof, "For Japan, A Quandary on Pleasing Two Giants," *New York Times*, August 24, 1997, p. 9, in *Lexis/Nexis*.
10. Cal Clark, "Changing Middle Class Constituencies and Party Competition on Taiwan: Implications for the Security Challenge," paper presented in the Conference on Dilemmas and Opportunity: Taiwan's National Security, Dallas, Texas, April 1998.
11. Taiwanization is a process began under President Chiang Ching-Kuo. This process involves bringing islanders into important positions in government and the KMT.
12. Cal Clark, "Changing Middle Class Constituencies," p.35.
13. This is a view strongly held by the DPP leadership and later the KMT itself.
14. Steve Chan, "Mirror, Mirror, on the Wall...Are the Freer Countries More Pacific?" *Journal of Conflict Resolution*, Vol. 28 (1984) pp. 617-664; Bruce Russett and Zeev Maoz, "Normative and Structural Causes of Democratic Peace, 1946-1986," *American Political Science Review*, Vol. 87, No. 3 (1993), pp. 624-638.
15. Steve Chan, *East Asian Dynamism: Growth, Order, and Security in the Pacific Region* (Boulder: Westview, 1990), p. 63.
16. Cal Clark, "Changing Middle Class Constituencies," pp. 38-40; see also Myra Lu, "Taiwan People Prefer Cross-Strait Status Quo," Taipei Journal, September 16, 2000, p. 1.
17. Robert Keohane, *After Hegemony* (Princeton: Princeton University Press, 1984).
18. Elizabeth Freund, "President Clinton's Three-No's and the Taiwan Question," *Working Paper in Taiwan Studies*, No. 32.
19. This status quo is a position that can be equated to a Nash equilibrium outcome. Though not exactly Pareto optimal from the perspective of PRC and Taiwan domestic politics, it is a equilibrium position that is non-provocative to all parties involved.
20. Current President Chen Shui-bian proposed a mini-direct link between Taiwan's outer islands of Kinmen, Matsu, and Penghu with the mainland province of Fujian to gradually reduce the tension between both sides of the Taiwan Straits.
21. For example, former President Lee Teng-hui in 1999 was quoted in an interview with *Deustche Welle* as stating that negotiations between the PRC and Taiwan should be based on a "special state to state" status. The United States and the PRC were swift to criticize this particular statement. The United States sent top emissaries to express Washington's displeasure with the statement's perception that it is an attempt by Taiwan to change or move away from the status quo. As a result of this interview, Washington and Beijing viewed President Lee Teng-hui as a troublemaker.
22. "Taiwan Tones Down Its War Games," *Reuters*, September 22, 2000.
23. Bates Gill and James Reilly, "Sovereignty, Intervention, and Peacekeeping: The View from Beijing," *Survival*, Vol. 42, No. 3 (Autumn 2000) p. 41.
24. Chan, *East Asian Dynamism*, p.112.
25. Ibid, p. 112.
26. American action in the area has shown that the status quo is its preferred position.

As a case in point, Washington's decision to send naval warships during the PRC's 1995 missile exercises off the coast of Taiwan is meant to deter any outbreak of open conflict between the two sides and disrupt the status quo. Similarly, Washington's decision to include Taiwan in the Theater Missile Defense is a clear signal that it prefers maintenance of the status quo in cross-Strait relations.

Index

For Product Safety Concerns and Information please contact our EU
representative GPSR@taylorandfrancis.com
Taylor & Francis Verlag GmbH, Kaufingerstraße 24, 80331 München, Germany

www.ingramcontent.com/pod-product-compliance
Lightning Source LLC
Chambersburg PA
CBHW050530270326
41926CB00015B/3149

9 781138 728028